METROPOLITAN ICONS

*Selected Poems of János Pilinszky
in Hungarian and in English*

János Pilinszky in the Mid-1960s

Photo by Károly Koffán

METROPOLITAN ICONS

*Selected Poems of János Pilinszky
in Hungarian and in English*

Edited and Translated by

Emery George

Studies in Slavic Language and Literature
Volume 8

The Edwin Mellen Press
Lewiston/Queenston/Lampeter

Library of Congress Cataloging-in-Publication Data

Pilinszky, János.
   [Poems. English & Hungarian. Selections]
   Metropolitan icons : selected poems of János Pilinszky in
Hungarian and in English / edited and translated by Emery George.
       p.   cm. -- (Studies in Slavic language and literature ; v. 8)
   Includes bibliographical references.
   ISBN 0-7734-9058-2
   1. Pilinszky, János--Criticism and interpretation. I. George,
Emery Edward, 1933-   . II. Title. III. Series.
PH3321.P46A6 1995
894'.51113--dc20   94-36506
                                                                          CIP

This is volume 8 in the continuing series
Studies in Slavic Language and Literature
Volume 8 ISBN 0-7734-9058-2
SSLL Series ISBN 0-88946-290-9

A CIP catalog record for this book is available from the British Library.

   The Edwin Mellen Press   The Edwin Mellen Press
          Box 450   Box 67
   Lewiston, New York   Queenston, Ontario
   USA 14092-0450   CANADA L0S 1L0

                   The Edwin Mellen Press, Ltd.
                      Lampeter, Dyfed, Wales
                   UNITED KINGDOM SA48 7DY

               Printed in the United States of America

In memoriam

L. H. G.

M. H. G.

CONTENTS

ACKNOWLEDGMENTS

My debts in connection with the present project are manifold and pleasant. My foremost thanks go to Péter Kovács, of Székesfehérvár, Hungary, the present heir to the literary rights of János Pilinszky. Dr. Kovács graciously granted me permission to publish in bilingual format the seventy-two poems by János Pilinszky and my translations of these poems included in this selection. In addition he provided me with invaluable information on persons and other matters elucidated in the Notes on the Poems. My warm thanks go, furthermore, to "Artisjus," the Literary, Theatrical, and Musical Agency of the Hungarian Bureau for the Protection of Authors' Rights, Budapest, in particular to Katalin Fodor, Dóra Károlyi, and Katalin Kátai, for putting me in touch with Dr. Kovács and providing further valuable help with the securing of rights. I also thank Károly Koffán, Jr., for his kind permission to use his father's photograph of the poet that appears as the frontispiece to our volume.

Among librarians and archivists I am deeply grateful to Dóra Csanak, Director, Manuscript Division, Hungarian Academy of Sciences, for assistance with archival Pilinszky materials; to István Papp, Deputy Director, Metropolitan Ervin Szabó Library, Budapest, for his kindness in sending me substantial bibliographic listings of holdings at his institution, as well as photocopies of scholarly sources; to the General and Humanities Reference Division, Princeton University Library, and to its able Head, Mary W. George, for frequent and complex bibliographic assistance; also to the Interlibrary Loan Services of Princeton University Library, for much-appreciated help with the securing of books and articles on interlibrary loan.

Institutions to which I am deeply indebted, either for assistance on visits or for books sent on interlibrary loan, include the libraries of: University of California, Berkeley; Columbia University (also its Music Library); Cornell University; Harvard University; Indiana University; The University of Michigan; State University College, Buffalo, New York; Princeton University (also Marquand Library of Art and Archaeology); Rutgers University; and Yale University. For similar kindnesses I also thank the Library of the Museum of Modern Art, New York, and the New York Public Library. Individuals in the

United States who have my thanks for information that was incorporated into either set of notes include Robert Austerlitz, Columbia University, and Mark Wiedenbeck, of Altadena, California.

While János Pilinszky is no longer an unknown poet in America, I was determined to make this a scholarly rather than a plain-text selection. I am gratefully indebted in particular to Tibor Tüskés, to date Pilinszky's only biographer, and to the editor of the poet's literary estate, István Jelenits. Equally valued is Endre Török's edition of Pilinszky's interviews.

Not last, my warm thanks go to the editors of magazines and anthologies, for publishing many of these translations and for permitting me to reprint them here, as follows:

Antigonish Review: "Admonition," "Cattle Brand," "Pietà";

Blue Unicorn: "Looking for the Prodigal Son," "The Rest Is Mercy," "The Seventh Circle of Hell";

Denver Quarterly: "Under a Winter Sky";

The Kenyon Review: "Love's Desert";

The Literary Review: "Definition," "From the Henchman's Diary," "Hölderlin," "Opening," "Two";

Mr. Cogito: "French Prisoner";

Nimrod: "Meetings";

Partisan Review: "Experience," "Holy Thief";

Poetry Now: "Elysium in November," "Introit," "Passion," "Ravensbrück Passion," "Van Gogh";

Southern Humanities Review: "Four-Liner," "The Henchman's Room," "Perpetuum mobile."

"Elysium in November," "Game," "Imperfect Tense" (under the title "A Past Half-Lived"), "A Little Night Music," "Two Portraits," and "Van Gogh" appeared in *New Directions in Prose and Poetry 42*.

"Enough," "For Jutta," "Noon," "Straight Labyrinth," "Through a Lifetime," and "To Two Lovers" first appeared in the anthology *The Age of Koestler*, edited by Nicolaus P. Kogon (Kalamazoo, MI: Practices of the Wind, 1994). Copyright © 1994 by Nicolaus P. Kogon.

"Afterword," "Celebration of Nadir," "Fragment from the Golden Age," and "Paraphrase" originally appeared, and were recently reprinted, in: *Contemporary East European Poetry: An Anthology*, edited by Emery George (Ann Arbor:

Ardis, 1983; New York, Oxford: Oxford University Press, 1993). Copyright © 1983 by Ardis Publishers. Reprinted by permission of Oxford University Press, Inc.

In closing I wish to express my kindest thanks to my publishers, The Edwin Mellen Press: to Professor Herbert Richardson, Director, and to Mr. John Rupnow, Managing Editor, for their encouragement of my work and for valuable assistance with a number of details that have helped make this a handsome and appealing book. To Mrs. Mitzie Kiszewski, of Niagara Falls, New York, I am deeply indebted for her great care with the preparation of the camera-ready copy.

Princeton, New Jersey   *—Emery George*
August 1994

INTRODUCTION

János Pilinszky first crossed my field of vision in Ann Arbor, in the late 1970s. My first volume of translations, *Subway Stops*, a selection of poems by Miklós Radnóti, had just appeared;[1] I was in the midst of translating a variety of Hungarian poets, among them Gyula Illyés, Lajos Kassák, Ottó Orbán, István Vas, and Sándor Weöres. As always, someone was missing. One fine October afternoon a colleague in East European Studies, hearing of my work, let fall the remark: What about János Pilinszky, often called the most distinguished poet of the postwar generation? That day I was hearing the name János Pilinszky for the first time in my life. My colleague immediately made some suggestions on poems: I should translate, among others, "Introit." I will be honest in recalling that I did not take to the poem on first reading. Pilinszky's native Roman Catholicism struck a foreign note, and it suggested periods of Western art that were not then and are still not my favorites: Carolingian illumination, the Book of Kells, Merovingian enamels. There was, in brief, temporary distrust of a mode to which I was not accustomed. Little did I suspect back then that I was being tested; that what is truly significant about János Pilinszky's poetry is that it is not written for our comfort. To understand it, we have to change.

Even in our age of minimalist verse, and to one who has read the work of Paul Celan, Pilinszky's art seemed strange enough at first. It was different, on its own terms: extraterrestrial, more to the point, extraterritorial, even un-Hungarian in its insistence on remembering. Few if any of the postwar Hungarian poets address themselves to the fates of those who perished in Hitler's camps. If they do sing of oppression, it is of the aftermath of the events of 1956, as does, for example, Ágnes Nemes Nagy in her poem "Ikhnaton's Night."[2] Yet it is also Nemes Nagy who recognizes how different a poet János Pilinszky is, and how fortunate contemporary Hungarian poetry is to have such a voice resonating with its many others. That national poetry needed one, but one among the many:

> ... to write the supreme poetry of the death camp experience. But that was not enough. Why was it just Pilinszky who could best tell the story of the scandal of the century, he who was not even present in it?

xvii

No, participation is not the key word, but identity, the preparedness from the start of his person for this very experience. This is where he is special, that is the nature of his otherness, beyond the periodic table; he recognised the death camp as his imaginings come true, the way a space-being recognizes the cold of space.[3]

Different is the word. In the great polygon of postwar Hungarian poetry, there are many intersecting radii, many divergent and overlapping talents. Kassák is the man of the isms, Illyés is the populist, Hajnal the hymnic singer of love, Weöres the anthropologist and linguist. As Nemes Nagy so aptly observes: "Everybody is different but some are even more so."[4] And, very soon, only Pilinszky truly stands to the side; he does not yield. A Catholic, agnostic, existentialist, and anti-fascist poet—anti-fascist, that is, before that stance came to be imposed from above—Pilinszky is not merely interested in the Holocaust. He is preoccupied with it; he dwells on it. He does not dutifully commiserate, then turn his attention to other matters of topical interest. He calls out to the heavens from the depths of his being; he lives and dies by his ability to say to the divine: "My God, my God, why hast thou forsaken me?" The cry of crucified humanity is what we hear and overhear in some of the best of this poet's work, from *On the Third Day* through *Crater*.

I

János Pilinszky was born in Budapest on 27 November 1921, and died there on 27 May 1981, just six months short of his sixtieth birthday. Of the generation that came to participate both in the tragedy of war and in the transition from the riches of interbellum to those of postwar Hungarian letters, Pilinszky was fortunate, yet born into modest circumstances. In his background, which, judging by the name, Tibor Tüskés believes to be Polish on the father's side,[5] there were some talented people: two of his four paternal uncles were distinguished operatic tenors. His father, a postmaster with a law degree, died tragically young after a mishandled operation for ulcers in 1937. After his death the young Pilinszky grew up among women: his mother, his sister, Veronika (nicknamed Erika), and three aunts. The Baitz family were originally from

Alsace-Lorraine. One of the three sisters of the poet's mother, Borbála (Bébi), had a speech impediment, and in addition never learned the language correctly. She taught Pilinszky to speak; in later life the poet, somewhat bemused, reflects that they taught each other. He has other interesting memories. Aunt Erzsébet co-founded and ran a convent-like correctional institution for teen-age prostitutes. Here, young János was a regular Sunday visitor, in his velvet finery a comical contrast to the adolescent girls in prison uniforms. This experience is vividly portrayed in the late poem "Sketch." In Pilinszky's comment on the world of children, he stresses the importance of the eye.[6]

All of Pilinszky's schooling took place in Budapest. In the fall of 1927, when the future poet was not yet six years old, his parents enrolled him in elementary school, and János proved to be an eager, good student. The eight years he spent in the piarist *gymnasium*—1931-1939—were under the tutelage of some outstanding teachers: of György Balanyi (history), Nándor Ohmacht (theology and ethics), and Imre Szita (mathematics and physics; Szita was also Pilinszky's form master). Here, the poet already showed himself the half recluse he was to become in later life. His grades were not always the best; he was better at sports than at major subjects, although he studied Latin and modern languages (French, German), and early showed keen interest in literature. Active membership in the school's student literary circle became important for him. His readings since elementary school days included the great Russian prose writers, Shakespeare and modern drama (Ibsen, Hauptmann, Pirandello), and poetry (Baudelaire, Ady). By his own lights, Pilinszky owes his beginnings as a poet to Endre Ady and to Attila József, although the entire côterie of distinguished writers clustered around the leading literary periodical *Nyugat* (Occident), with Mihály Babits at their helm, would prove decisive for Pilinszky's development. What was important to him from the beginning was to celebrate the world, but not the obvious in it, and to be a poet not for a living, but rather as a mode of being.[7]

Pilinszky's first published poem, "Anyám" ("My Mother"), appeared early, in the May 1938 issue of *Élet* (Life).[8] With this debut he came into contact with key figures of publicistic and literary life, among them the highly active Gábor Thurzó, who also worked on the editorial boards of the short-lived *Ezüstkor* (Silver Age) and of the distinguished and long-lived liberal Catholic monthly *Vigilia* (founded in 1935). The last-named became hospitable to Pilinszky's work in February of 1939. Among other periodicals to which the poet came to contribute relatively early are *Diárium* (Diary), *Magyarok* (Hungarians), *Újhold* (New Moon), and *Válasz* (Reply). Of particular importance for Pilinszky was early acceptance of his work on the pages of *Magyar Csillag* (Hungarian Star), under the editorial guidance of Illyés a worthy direct successor to *Nyugat*. The point of succession is marked by Babits's death in August of 1941; by this time war and bad times were coming on the country. After but three issues (of March, June, and September 1943) *Ezüstkor* was banned as a haven for "many a suspect element," as was, in time, *Magyar Csillag* itself, shortly after the German occupation of Hungary in March of 1944. Besides these magazines, the old school publication *Piarista Öregdiák* (Piarist Alumnus) remained hospitable to Pilinszky's poems long after he had become a student at the Péter Pázmány University. Pilinszky graduated from the latter on 13 May 1944, although he never took his doctorate; his dissertation, along with other writings and family papers, was destroyed during the siege of Budapest of 1944-1945.[9]

For reasons of health and schooling Pilinszky received several deferments from military service; his call-up, in November of 1944, was one of the last before the end of World War II. With his unit the poet moved west, and there he had the privilege of experiencing the remnants of wartime horrors, in particular the world of the extermination camps. It was at one time or another thought that he himself had been interned in one or more of them. Tüskés relates that when Pilinszky was confronted with the question, with oracular calm he would say: "It's so much beside the point! Tolstoy did not participate in the Napoleonic wars, either!"[10] There is, however, a slight difference between the degree of participation of the two writers. Pilinszky did see what he wrote about, and left eyewitness accounts of what he saw. And experiences that were to become explicit subjects of poems extend not "only" to the camps, but also to personal travail elsewhere out west, especially in Germany. This applies particularly to "Frankfurt" and to "Apocrypha." The eyewitness motif is most shockingly direct, of course, in the poems on specific camps: in "Harbach 1944," "French Prisoner," "On a KZ Lager's Wall," "Ravensbrück Passion," and "On the Third Day." It would be tempting to try to dismiss the horrifying imagery of these works as products of a talented poetic mind guided by the news. We cannot; Tüskés cites but one example:

At the end of April, during the last days of the war, they arrive at Harbach.

His unit is stationed near an airport. They have no weapons; on the airport's runway they are to fill the bomb craters sunk by the English and American fliers, so that the German planes can take off. They do the work together with Belgian camp inmates; here is where he first meets inhabitants of the death camps.[11]

Pilinszky was lucky; after a serious illness—swollen legs, no medicine—he came to a UNRRA (United Nations Relief and Rehabilitation Agency) camp near Frankfurt. Here, he recovered—and also witnessed the horrors recorded in the poem named for the destroyed city. Yes, Pilinszky, the moment's "soldier of fortune," went through it all, saw it all—and became a totally transformed human being and poet. It would be a mistake to look to models first. To be sure, as Tüskés points out, Ady, Rilke, and Baudelaire are hereby poets of an overcome past; Attila József, with his poetic of anxiety, is the new model. Far more to the point is the inner poetic, the stance Pilinszky himself does his best to articulate in his essay "Instead of an *ars poetica*":

> Today, Auschwitz is a museum. Within its walls, the past—and in a certain sense, the past that belongs to every one of us—is here present with that infinite weight and that plainness that is at all times reality's innermost virtue; and for its doors having been closed, it has become more real, more valid still. ...
>
> All that happened here is scandal insofar as it *could* happen, and sacred without exception insofar as it *did* happen.
>
> All this is true. And yet it is tortuously contradictory and, if anywhere, it is here that the dialogue of the Karamazovs is lent weight. Alyosha's faith; and Ivan's rebelliousness, cloaking itself in indifference.[12]

It should not surprise us if two of Pilinszky's guiding spirits in the mature poetry should be Dostoyevsky, creator of the Karamazovs and the possessed, and that most baffling of modern hagiographic phenomena, Simone Weil.[13]

Pilinszky was away from home for one year; he arrived back in Budapest in November 1945. With enthusiasm he rejoined the regenerating literary life of the capital, although in 1944 he wrote no poems, and in 1945 and 1946, but two each (respectively: "Belated Grace" and "I'm Telling You"; and "Harbach 1944" and "Because You Were Soaking Wet, Were Cold").[14] Pilinszky's first volume of poetry, *Trapéz és korlát* (Trapeze and Parallel Bars), appeared in the summer of 1946, under the Ezüstkor imprint. Almost immediately it won the recognition of leading critics,[15] despite the fact that the slim volume contains but nineteen poems (organized in three cycles), the product of the years 1940-1946. Pilinszky never was a prolific poet, and this fact has elicited comment from friends, colleagues, and critics alike. When, for example, László Cs. Szabó conducted his first interview with the poet in London in 1967, he asked, point-blank: "Why do you write so little?" Pilinszky's answer: "A good sonnet is not shorter than *War and Peace.*" Then he added (and this reply is by far the better known and the more often quoted): "What is important is not how many times a bird beats with its wings, but that it should soar."[16]

Pilinszky's eagle of poetic flight did beat with its wings relatively few times and it did soar, despite the fact that, like other writers of his generation, he too underwent censure and silencing during the Stalinist years. Between spring 1949 and summer 1956 he was forbidden to publish verse;[17] when his second volume, *Harmadnapon* (On the Third Day), appeared in 1959, it contained but thirty-three new poems. *Nagyvárosi ikonok* (Metropolitan Icons) (1970, [2]1971) contains even fewer as the product of the intervening decade—only fifteen new poems, and the longer "KZ Oratorio." During this middle period Pilinszky seems to be writing less and less. While between the years 1941 and 1958 his annual average was three poems, between 1959 and 1970 he writes fewer than one per year.[18] If, as has been believed, this points to a crisis of poetic identity, the critics either do not notice or do not misunderstand. To them Pilinszky is and remains a first-class poet concerned with ultimate questions and stressing quality rather than quantity. This latter distinction is deceptive; the quantity is there, but it is not in numbers of poems alone that we are to seek it.

Quantity in the sense of productivity becomes a reality for Pilinszky at the start of the 1970s. *Metropolitan Icons* was to be followed by three final volumes of verse: *Szálkák* (Splinters) (1972), *Végkifejlet* (Dénouement) (1974), and *Kráter* (Crater) (1976). In them the number of poems undergoes dramatic increase. The fourth and fifth volumes are no longer *Collected*s, as were the second and the third; and the poems in the three total 146 (1972: 58; 1974: 38; 1976: 50). The method of these last poems also changes radically; in *Crater*, for example, poems of two or three lines are not at all uncommon (e.g., "Pascal," "Two," "Hölderlin," "Temptation"). It is almost as if in these texts the poet were being replaced by the epigrammatist, or the writer of verse aphorisms. Be that as it may, the slender yet ample poetic oeuvre of 214 collected poems speaks for itself. Nor is Pilinszky unproductive in other genres. Additional volumes include three of verse tales for children; uncollected poems and verse translations, including a portion of Hugo von Hofmannsthal's *Elektra*; four minimalist plays collected in *Dénouement*; and the film script *Rekviem* (Requiem) (1964). His voluminous occasional prose, first published mostly in the Catholic weekly *Új Ember* (New Man), of which Pilinszky was contributing editor from 1 November 1957, has been available since 1984 in two hefty volumes under the title *A mélypont ünnepélye* (Celebration of Nadir). Finally there are interviews and conversations, both real and imaginary, among them *Beszélgetések Sheryl Suttonnal* (Conversations with Sheryl Sutton), this last title also available in English translation.[19]

In time international recognition came to the poet, and a great deal of it manifested itself in invitations to visit abroad—in travel. Already in 1947-1948 he had spent several months in Italy as a fellow of the Hungarian Academy in Rome, and also visited Switzerland; in 1963 he spent the summer in France. It is from this visit that Pilinszky's acquaintance with both Pierre Emmanuel and the writings of Simone Weil dates.[20] Further half-year study trips to Western Europe came in 1967, when Pilinszky sojourned in Vienna, Paris, Belgium, London, and Rome; and in 1970 to Paris, the latter at the invitation of the Catholic existentialist philosopher Gabriel Marcel. Lecture invitations came in 1972 to the Sorbonne and in 1975 to New York, where Pilinszky lectured at Columbia University. The ever-increasing number of his travels since the early 1960s took him to such far-flung places as Sweden and Tunisia; in 1965, to Poland (with his sister, to Częstochowa and to Oświęcim), and at the end of the year to Switzerland, in the company of Sándor Weöres and Amy Károlyi. Tüskés relates how, in Berne, the three poets admired the childlike art of Paul Klee; and how in Neuchâtel they were guests of Friedrich Dürrenmatt, who held forth on his latest work and on the poetics of film and theater. Pilinszky's visit to the Carthusian monastery at Valsainte is commemorated in his poem "After Confession."[21]

Stimulating and augmenting as these travels no doubt were, none probably meant more to the poet than the four distinct occasions—in 1969, 1972, 1976, and 1980—when in England he had opportunities to meet fellow poets from the English-speaking world. The 1969 and 1972 visits were guest appearances at Poetry International, London, where poets of the stature of W. H. Auden, Robert Bly, Robert Creeley, and Ted Hughes were also present. There was magic in the air; Pilinszky did not speak a word of English, Hughes not a word of Hungarian, and yet they communicated, somehow. The year 1976 marked the appearance, with the Carcanet New Press, Manchester, of Pilinszky's *Selected Poems*, in the collaborative translation by Ted Hughes and János Csokits.[22] Pilinszky's poems have been translated regularly since the end of the 1970s; translations into a number of European languages have been appearing in magazines, anthologies, individual volumes, and as sound recordings, a way of preserving his work that the poet especially prized.[23] While it seems true that Pilinszky's work is as translatable as that of any other world-class poet, it is an exaggeration to say, as does Tüskés, that "he is the contemporary Hungarian poet who has succeeded with the best results ... in breaking through the 'airless isolation' that surrounds our literature."[24] Similar claims can be made for Ady, Kassák, József, Radnóti, and Weöres. Still, this is not bad company. To cite but one further sign of recognition: poems by Pilinszky have been set to music by the Hungarian composer György Kurtág; his *Four Songs to Poems by János Pilinszky*, opus 11, sets "Alcohol," "In memoriam F. M. Dostoyevsky," "Hölderlin," and "Beating."[25]

In the end it is the artist as a human being who places the full stop at the close of his own life sentence. If Pilinszky started out as a recluse, he did not remain one. There are photographs of him showing him smiling and laughing.[26] Fellow intellectuals remember him as concerned for others, eager to communicate, to listen and to help, and especially to give interviews. As time went on he was also increasingly concerned about his health. Everyone, not last the poet himself, felt his "accelerating time," and the need affectionately to help him close his book. In 1980 Pilinszky was awarded the third and greatest of his public distinctions at home: after the Baumgarten (1947) and Attila József (1971) Prizes, the coveted Kossuth Prize, for lifetime achievement in letters. His death, in Budapest on 27 May 1981, was caused by a sudden heart attack. He was buried, at Farkasrét Cemetery, on 4 June.[27]

"[Pilinszky] wrote only his selected works; he did not leave the task of winnowing his poems to posterity."[28] This is a highly accurate observation. Opening *Collected Poems* to the first book, *Trapeze and Parallel Bars*, we receive an impression of economy, leanness; of a tight, muscular poetry totally adequate to the gymnastic suggestions of the first book's title. The poems are turned toward the speaking persona and, often, toward a reality addressed as well. The lyric "I" explores at least three possibilities of encounter with self and with the world: "You Be the One to Defeat Me" is addressed to the night; in "Midnight Bath" the poet is alone, with birds in flight over a lake; "Fish in a Net" confronts our universal human condition; in "To Myself," the self is exhorted not to leave its fate to the stars, and in the end turns invisible even to the addressing persona.

In the middle of the collection there is a great deal more on stars, also on a sense of existing off limits, on forbidden territory. A good example is the eloquent poem whose title unites the two concerns: "On a Forbidden Star"; here, the poet sees himself not only as having been born on such a heavenly body, but also as having been "pursued ashore" (line 2). This self-image is then developed further in the title poem; the poet sees both himself and his loved one exiled from and yet gymnastically working out toward "wing-beating reality" (line 17). In the end we, poet and lover, "sit on heaven's parallel bars, / like sentenced convicts." Finally, "Under a Winter Sky" sees the poet back with the self, irremediably alone and defenseless (stanzas 1, 4, and 5):

> Over my head the stars
> mix icy fire;
> under the merciless sky I fall
> supine against the wall.
>
> ...
>
> I'll deceive myself no longer:
> there's no one around to help me,
> no suffering will redeem,

no god will protect me.

Nothing could be simpler
than this, nothing more monstrous.
Slowly they start out toward me:
the biblical monsters. (17-18; 5)[29]

There is still a touch of childlike simplicity, if not of emotion then of means, about this confessional piece; in telling contrast, the key poem "Because You Were Soaking Wet, Were Cold" is accomplished technically as well. The latter takes it up directly where "Under a Winter Sky" left off, with an image of "monsters" (line 2), and yet the new text alludes in its self-examining agony to specific historic events: "because you were soaking wet, were cold, / because in me you knew hunger, / though I was soaked and cold myself, / and had nothing to eat, either" (lines 13-16). The game is up; from this text the poet's vision arches over to nothing less monstrous than the abhorrent hunger-and-garbage imagery of a major poem like "Frankfurt." Existential agony is the note on which the opening book closes, on an eloquent poem like "What Sort of Underground Struggle" (which is not without its own touches of realism: there are images of cigarette, gray hair, bloodshot eyes, straw sack, the taste of hell in one's mouth); and yet the poem that precedes it is titled "Fear Not."

The reader coming to Pilinszky's art from the free-verse, Pléïade, and classical splendors of some of the best interbellum Hungarian poets (e.g., of Füst, Kosztolányi, Radnóti) and expecting similar virtuosity will be disappointed. Pilinszky's prosodic means are spare and limited, remaining for the most part confined to a basic iambic beat[30] and a four-line strophic unit, else couplet, however many times repeated per stanza (as, e.g., in "Fish in a Net" or in "Midnight Bath"). These means then achieve, for all their limitations, impressive effects of rhythm and energy by the skilful use of enjambement and by the insistent repetition of a basic metrical unit (as in "Stigma"). For Pilinszky, denying himself brilliant prosodic display was important; his increasing spareness is surely an aspect of his self-consciously Catholic and existential asceticism. Not that it is not clear that a poet sees no separation between what he has to say and the form the material takes, from within. But for Pilinszky, what is to be communicated comes first, and the order and level of prosodic realization is a function of the urgency with which the poem does its verbal job of singing and portraying. Pilinszky's portraits are drypoint etchings; his enterprise begins at a point of muted if variable control rooted in the tradition of the dramatic monologue. What is omitted soon gives itself away in the changes that the poems are to undergo; the technical limitation of the early work is itself an aspect of this poet's problematic silence.

Trapeze and Parallel Bars originally contained nineteen poems; the eighteen (three cycles of six poems each) we see in *Collected Poems* is explained by the fact that Pilinszky later decided to take out "Harbach 1944" and to make it the opening piece of the second cycle of his second book, *On the Third Day*.[31] Like its successor, *Metropolitan Icons*, this second collection is divided into but two cycles, of unequal length, the first of these perhaps predictably continuing the subject-object *trobar clus* of the first book. Here, in the cycle *In No Man's Land*, we encounter almost regular alternation of "I" and "you" poems: "Paraphrase" versus "Sin," "Without Witnesses" versus the adjacent "To Two Lovers," "World Grown Cold" versus "Pietà."[32] Yet another significant nexus between *Trapeze and Parallel Bars* and *On the Third Day* is the language of "In No Man's Land," in some ways strongly reminiscent of that of "On a Forbidden Star."[33] The poet's vocabulary is here already defining itself; that "crater of the throbbing pupil" ("In No Man's Land," line 14) takes us straight to the late poem "Crater." It should come as no surprise to see the old title of "KZ Oratorio," "Dark Heaven," figure in the poetry as early as the closing line of "You Be the One to Defeat Me," the opening poem of *Trapeze and Parallel Bars*. Every poet has his or her characteristic lexicon, and Pilinszky is no exception. Careful reading reveals certain repetition patterns that can be identified as aspects of the poet's style.[34]

It is in the second book, *On the Third Day*, that the self-imposed limitations of the earlier work—"I" versus "you" poetry, subjectivity, the insistent confessional mode—either share the stage with or yield to that cry of the heart without which there is no definitive achievement by János Pilinszky. Headed by "Harbach 1944," the poem he rescued over from *Trapeze and Parallel Bars*, the second cycle of *On the Third Day* contains the greatest concentration of Pilinszky's war and Holocaust poetry. No fewer than seven major poems, the first six in quick succession, occur here alone: "Harbach 1944," "French Prisoner," "On a KZ Lager's Wall," "Ravensbrück Passion," "On the Third

Day," Frankfurt"; coming somewhat later but still in the second collection, "Apocrypha."[35] From this point on we are attending to the compelling world of the artist who dare say the unsayable. Here is the opener of "Harbach 1944":

> Again and again I see them:
> bright moon and a shaft, hard,
> and, harnessed to the shaft, men
> pull an enormous cart. (39; 21)

In the end, the men die. The powerful imagery reminds us of the work of that other Holocaust poet, Anthony Hecht, who in his collection *The Hard Hours* asks: "Who now remembers 'The Singing Horses of Buchenwald'?"[36] As if Pilinszky did not make us remember enough. He himself is personally filled with specific remembrance ("French Prisoner"):

> I glance into my notes and quote the line:
> "Could I but forget that one, the Frenchman ... ."
> And out my ears, my eyes, my mouth,
> fiery memory yells at me, singeing:
>
> "I'm hungry!" And suddenly I feel
> the hunger that cannot and will not die,
> which the wretch has not felt for so long,
> and which no earthly food will satisfy.
> He lives on me! And ever hungrier!
> And for him I am ever the smaller part!
> He, who would have survived on any food,
> now returns to claim my very heart. (41; 27)

And this is the secret of Pilinszky's interest in the Holocaust—that it is not merely interest but involvement, the kind that claims the whole person, to the point of self-immersion, self-sacrifice. Much later, in "Cattle Brand," he formulates the stance with high precision: "Nail hammered into the world's palm, / I'm deathly pale. / Blooddrenched" (*Splinters*; 102; 147). In Pilinszky's vision the Holocaust is humanity crucified. In his feuilleton piece on Oświęcim, the poet writes of Edith Stein, the saintly Carmelite nun who died at Auschwitz, and who as a farewell message wrote: "'from the depth of my heart I cried out: Ave Crux, Spes Unica!'"[37] So Pilinszky cries out, and the first five of the poems on the Holocaust included in *On the Third Day*: "Harbach 1944," "French Prisoner," "On a KZ Lager's Wall," "Ravensbrück Passion," and "On the Third Day," record the cry. And in "Passion" the poet writes, against the eagerness of half of Europe to forget: "In silence behind glass / the butcher's assistants wash up, / but even so, somehow, what took place just cannot come to an end" (73; 107). Indeed it cannot.

Going on to develop the theme of history stated in the Holocaust verse, but in the dimensions of personal reminiscence, are two longer poems, "Frankfurt" and "Apocrypha." On a chessboard of eight times eight lines "Frankfurt" moves its pieces to checkmate, to year zero, a time of destruction and hunger:

> sharing in the fat of kitchen leavings,
> oh yes: forced onto all fours, hunger
> could scarcely stand its very own onslaught—
> and it rebelled, and straightaway surrendered. (43; 33)

At the poem's end we know precisely what that date—"*1945*"—signifies; the ruins, the desolation, inside and out: "the heat, fainting from among the gardens, / and, collapsing on us, loneliness" (44; 35). "Apocrypha" is a work of much the same temper, yet far more personal in its treatment of the theme of universal doom. It is the story of the return of the poet home, after the war; he sees himself as the Prodigal Son, "as he too arrived in the Bible." In this longer poem, in three sections, we are invited to recognize Biblical allusions, not last to Revelation; to attend to destroyed nature and to personal suffering; and to sympathize with an affecting familial scene (in section 2):

> My ghastly shadow in the courtyard.
> Careworn silence, old parents in the house.
> And now they come, and they call me, the poor dears
> cry now, they embrace me, stumbling.
> The old order receives me back.
> I prop my elbows on the windswept stars ... . (49; 49)

Yet the return is only partial; that image of bravado, of elbows propped on windswept stars, is deceptive. "Under the infrared of an angry sky," equipped with no more than a prison uniform and a walking stick, the speaker takes his "belated, bitter steps." He comes home, to his beloved, only to find himself bereft of speech, and disoriented by as much as "a garden chair, a deck chair left outside." The images of section 3 are those of ageing, of quiet despair, and of a note of impossibility, sounded in the closing conceit of the trickling of an empty ditch.

Poetry of the luminosity of the Holocaust pieces and of the personal writing is akin to photography—it is bare, silent. Confirming this feeling, "KZ Oratorio" is one of Pilinszky's minimalist plays, along with the film script *Requiem* one of his two major statements on the moral catastrophe of our time. Originally entitled "Sötét mennyország" ("Dark Heaven"),[38] "KZ Oratorio" comes as the third poem in *Metropolitan Icons*, following the two weighty poems "Afterword" and "Introit." In genre the "Oratorio" is a dramatic recitative written for presentation on stage, yet consciously aiming at a feeling of irreality. The work comes with silent orchestra and chorus, special lighting effects, and but three speaking participants. Tüskés is, I think, somewhat unfair to this major work, as he writes: "The oratorio is built of already well-known motifs lifted from the poems. Its vocabulary is the same as that of the poems: nails, ice-empty stars, night, dark corridor, prison garment, etc. ... But while these motifs, verbal images, and metaphors build in the poems into organic lyric work, become completed and turn into artistic wholes, here in the oratorio they remain fragments and raise the impression of a loose wall, piled up without binding agent."[39]

We can try to do the "Oratorio" justice by viewing it from the standpoint of the creative process, and of genre. That Pilinszky himself viewed the work simultaneously as poetry and as drama is clear; equally clear is the fact that he *wrote* the work, conceiving it carefully, and did not merely compile it from material taken from some of the previous poetry. That earlier lexicon should be visible in it is nonetheless logical, not to say inevitable. But while words thus tie the new experiment to the older writing, a part of what makes "KZ Oratorio" unique is that it departs from the aims and limitations of the five previous major Holocaust poems. There, what mattered was the recording of personal encounters. As we have already pointed out, Pilinszky actually met the prisoners of Harbach, and the poem "French Prisoner" captures immediacy of a highly similar order. The earlier poems, all in *On the Third Day*, may to an extent be called biographical. From the "Oratorio" biography is systematically excluded, and in place of the earlier approach we have a powerful work of the imagination.

"KZ Oratorio" is a dramatized post-mortem memoir by three inmates at an unnamed German concentration camp, one that Pilinszky did not know, perhaps Belsen or Dachau. There is here a difference from the film script *Requiem*. The camp in question, as the text more than once reminds us, is located in Germany. Of the three inmates, only the two women know where they are from; the little boy has forgotten. All the horrors are carefully rehearsed in the three characters' speeches, but with the exception of Germany no locale, no room at their destination, is named by name:

> OLD WOMAN
> It was just like a greenhouse,
> only there were no flowers in it.
> A single long corridor;
> adobe walls, but with earth's warmth.
> At its end the corridor widened,
> and gave off light, like a monstrance. (62; 77)

There is no need for specific naming; we have graphic clarity instead. Can we doubt that she is referring to the gas chamber? Attenuated and subtle as it is, this is the answer to the young boy's question, asked two speeches later: "We're dead, aren't we?" And when the little boy himself speaks of the "seven cubes" (64; 83), how can we possibly fail to see a string of boxcars? This can only mean that Pilinszky, a master of metaphor, intended "KZ Oratorio" to be understood as poetry, in addition to its status as drama.

The drama comes through unforgettably. The almost catatonic single-line speeches, many of them little more than nouns or noun phrases, strike a deeply right note; these people communicate without for a moment intending to do so. At the same time this is self-conscious theater; everyone knows the cast are on exhibit. As fellow travelers in the boxcar that brought them to the camp, as fellow sufferers of the humiliations of reception and processing horrors, they are clearly reduced to half silence. What is there to say? And yet speak they must, even if not—or rarely—to one another. No one addresses the young boy; occasionally the girl and the old woman exchange lines that sound like dialogue. There is the subject of love; Hungarian being genderless in its third-person pronouns, the original text does markedly less than the translation in conveying the girl's sense of the nearness of her young man (64-65; 83, 85). The principals, then, manage to communicate about as effectively as do characters in a Chekhov play. The speeches, "recitatives," are mostly isolated lines or groups of lines. The more substantial portions, the "arias," are few and far between, such as the girl's tale of the pure-hearted wolf (62; 77, 79), or the boy's closing aria on the need for love:

> Unhappy the moment when
> the orphan discovers himself,
> and takes thought that this hand, this curve
> could also be important for another,
> and from then on he longs to be loved. (69; 95)

"KZ Oratorio" shares with the poems of *Metropolitan Icons* the condition of standstill. My choice of a title for the present selection adverts to the iconic immobility of Pilinszky's art.[40] Once the reader is caught in the labyrinth of this poetry, there seems to be no way out. Yet the verse also sings of hope. Beyond the Holocaust opus the poems of *On the Third Day* and *Metropolitan Icons* are a shared realm, of a new and engaging competence, and of a variable and complex tone. One of the big surprises of *On the Third Day* is "Fragment from the Golden Age." Coming immediately after "Frankfurt," it strikes an unexpectedly happy, even euphoric, note, as if it meant to say: "Enough of the mourning; there is also such a thing as being comforted, even if with reserve, even if chaos still rules the scene in part." The closing stanza is a celebration of the sun:

> What emerges here, from this sea of radiance?
> Even when I close them, it burns my eyes;
> what outside is white-hot—inside the pupil
> is where it's incandescent: here, inside!

It's only with it the world turns bright,
of joy, which is always shy of a name.
As at a gallows, so blinding it is,
and so sweet. It's how all things are made. (45; 39)

Note the bittersweet blend of "joy" and "gallows," of "bright" and "blinding,"
the caution, but also the acceptance. Perhaps it is also a time for healing. This
is precisely what is depicted in the closing piece of the second book, "Elysium
in November"; the poet seems to be addressing a friend:

> ... , as though anointed with holy oil,
> your senses' five tortured wounds
> feel relief and healing.
>
> You are shy and jubilant! Yes,
> with your limbs, translucent as a child's,
> in the overgrown scarf and topcoat,
> you are just like Alyosha Karamazov. (53; 61)

Dostoyevsky is one of Pilinszky's four or five closest affinities (see also the
two Stavrogin poems, in *Dénouement*), along with the Bible, Simone Weil, Van
Gogh (to whose work the poet devotes two poems, both of them translated here)
and, by implication in the poetry (discussed in the prose), J. S. Bach.[41]
Continuing, in *Metropolitan Icons*, with the depiction of wary, conditional
acceptance of what cannot be changed, Pilinszky tries a surreal serenade, as in
"A Little Night Music"; the poem is dated "*Paris, 1963*." Its music is not at all
dissimilar to that of "KZ Oratorio"; in the closing section, "*Mozart*," we hear:

> A house, a courtyard. My dream and my death.
> Southern silence, memory.
> Searchlight-gleam on the walls,
> emptiness and marble veins.
>
> "Dans cette maison habita Mozart" –
> Mozart lived here once.

In a vase a bouquet of flowers.

O gallows-fragrance! (72; 103)

In later books, the gallows motif is touched on again. Already now, in *Metropolitan Icons*, we are treated to similar smells and sights: in "From the Henchman's Diary," although with the glance turned away and replaced by a great moment of ambiguity and silence; and in "Holy Thief," in which we know precisely where we find ourselves:

By then the flies had covered him

beyond agony,
beyond tetanus,
and far beyond nails, wounds, ... (74; 111)

"friend, / friendship forever." The friendship of the Redeemer—that is the panel on which this collection of metropolitan icons closes. As in the title poem, so here Pilinszky's music of recovery and return reminds us of the poet's point of view that we are entitled to our humanity because God took on human form; and that if we suffer and recover it is because he suffers but does not, short of doing so "beyond tetanus, / and far beyond nails, wounds, ..." That word "beyond" holds the key.

In "Holy Thief" a silent allusion to the Passion oratorios of J. S. Bach is unmistakable. Music is an appropriate adjunct to—and, on occasion, a structural dimension of—the three early books; whether the outward reference is to Mozart or the inward one to Bach, the music is first of all that of the poems. Starting with *Splinters*, there comes about a big change—the music is increasingly replaced by silence. Much has been made of Pilinszky's growing silent in his work, and he himself carved a discursive poetic out of his own awareness of the invitations and dangers of simply ceasing to write or even to speak.[42] This is not what I am referring to here. It is telling that, as Tüskés points out, growing silent in the sense of writing less and less was a danger to the poet in the 1950s, when silence was imposed from without, and in the 1960s, when Pilinszky voluntarily wrote, on the average, less than one poem per year. The fifteen new poems (besides "KZ Oratorio") of *Metropolitan Icons* show exactly this trend.[43] No—lack of productivity is not what we mean by the silence of the last three books. On the contrary, the number of poems increases dramatically, as we have pointed out before. What is silent about the books from *Splinters* through *Crater* is the poem itself.

Not that this new silence is all that new in Pilinszky's work as a whole; in the second book alone there are six poems containing no more than four lines apiece.[44] There is "Four-Liner," immediately following "Apocrypha":

Sleeping nails in the ice-cold sand.
Nights soaking in poster-solitude.
You left the light on in the hallway.
Today they are shedding my blood. (51; 55)

This is a poem to which Tüskés and other critics devote rather ample space.[45] Doubtless they are right. The poem is a puzzler; it is one of questioned and renewed imagery and, through the overriding image of the Passion, transferred to the personal sphere in line 4, a poem of renewed hope as well. But it is also more; "Four-Liner" does not accomplish its mission without a most important device, that of poetic silence.

The paratactic syntax of the four lines reminds Tüskés of "the stuck frames that interrupt the rolling of a film."[46] Such an observation stresses the visual; silence being an auditory matter, it also adverts to ways in which the poem is written. Is it accident that each of these four lines is a sentence? I think not. Those line-terminal full stops draw in their wake thunderous silences. Taking them at face value and not concerned with biographical intimations,[47] we concentrate on the world the poem evokes. These are cold nights, with the door left open. Someone has gone out, having negligently left a light on. The poet stands in the hallway, waiting. Yet he is not waiting for Godot, the person who never comes. With complete nonchalance he announces a scheduled event. Oh yes: they will come for him, as they come for the lamb in the closing line of "The Henchman's Room." The understatement of the Passion in "Four-Liner" is in perfect consonance with the big-city bleakness of the scene. As Béla Pomogáts has so aptly observed, there is no nature to speak of in Pilinszky's poetry; there is at all times the dreadful, cold desolation of the city.[48] Yet there is a redeeming feature in this minimalist vision; the image of the poet's blood, about to be shed, points to a fourfold path, a path on which not one physical step may be taken. Standing. Shivering. Keeping silent. Waiting. That is the path to salvation.

Whether the poems of the last three books agree with this philosophy of the fourfold path depends, of course, on the individual text, but they seem to agree for the most part. Like any other true artist, Pilinszky seeks ways to fulfill his art. These last poems bring us to the varieties of silence, to ways in which the urge to fulfillment records that astonishing inward voice. It happens in "The Henchman's Room" (*Splinters*), whose affinity with "Four-Liner" commends it to our attention. Like the latter, "The Henchman's Room" is a brief, four-sentence, poem ending on the image of the shedding of the blood of the Son of Man (line 6 "the lamb"). Here too images are stripped to their barest minimum; they are static and reductive, as in a dream, and as deeply charged with meaning. Yet there is one additional effect that recommends surreal status for the poem as a whole:

> Bacon smell. Geranium smell.
> You never see the sea from the window of the henchman's room.
> The sea belongs to God,
> and the window is closed. (91; 121)

As viewed from the henchman's room, the sea is none of our business. That we are not permitted to see the sea because it is God's property is a point we may understand also in the absence of images; it could be viewed purely as a theological matter. Had the poet ended the first stanza with line 3, we could conclude this, and none the wiser. But no—as poet he had to go on, completing the inner image of situation by adding an outer one of physical impossibility. Note that Pilinszky is not saying: "and the window is shuttered," or: "and the blinds are drawn." He writes a peremptory pair of lines, an equivalent of "End of subject." We cannot help feeling a tiny bit intimidated by the tone alone. We could come back another day, during hours when the window is open. Yet testiness is not all; the poet wants us to remain on our toes. The surreal effect of the suggestion that you cannot see the sea because the window is closed (albeit we are talking about transparent glass and perfectly clear visibility) casts its spell over the entire poem. Once again this effect is not totally new in Pilinszky's art; recall only the following lines from "Metropolitan Icons": "We start out toward a pile of stones, / and from behind it a bird flies up." In the vision of René Magritte, the bird itself would be of stone.[49]

The visual dimension of deep silence within the minimalist poem accounts for but a segment of its workings; equally real are the auditory realizations of all that may remain unsaid. Here are the closing two lines of "Crime and Punishment":

It's still summer.

Lower your scepter, Queen. (93; 123)

For a moment disregarding the question of what the poem has to do with the dedicatee, the actress Sheryl Sutton, and in the spirit of old-fashioned commentary, let us listen to the lacuna between these last two lines. It is filled with the hums of faraway summer, its drumming and music; with summer knowledge, as Delmore Schwartz would call it.[50] But Pilinszky tells us it is even more: it is the overheard knowledge of the faraway, of air and sun, of all that is audible because it is too far to be heard; the knowledge of beaches, of children, of running and play, of sailboats, and of ships far out on the open sea. All these strains are heard in that lacuna, including quiet intimations of Pilinszky's own summer vacations on Lake Balaton. But we learn: it's *still* summer, summer is still on; in other words, at any moment now, it may begin declining toward autumn: "Lower your scepter, Queen." And when from this concert of silent and faraway music, this humming of being, we come to "Admonition," but four poems over in *Splinters*, we understand how all of Pilinszky's work is a single indivisible body. Silence of both the visual and the acoustical species leads to the species spoken silence, to the spelling out of what is at the same time best left unspoken: "The hook's silence: note that" (Admonition," line 5). In the poem immediately following, "Gallows in Winter," we come to a place where silence takes the form of insistent statements: "I don't know"; "We know nothing." We are more than a little reminded of the speechless walls and clattering weather vanes in the closing lines of Hölderlin's "Hälfte des Lebens."[51]

The poet's game is one of resourcefulness. In *Dénouement* we have the silence of the dead, looking busy ("Game"), of the poem sliced in two ("Stavrogin Says Goodbye," "Stavrogin Returns"); in *Crater*, the silence of the stunning visual image of hell ("Spaces"); finally, silence of the special case, perhaps the most special in poetry, of a life told in three pregnant lines ("Hölderlin"). The Dostoyevsky poems and "Hölderlin" confirm us in our hunch that in Pilinszky's practice the poetological triad, with the silence of the visual image and the silence of music, is completed in the peculiarly silent dramatic monologue that is this late, three-line, text's own domain. We must go back a bit and recall "French Prisoner," "Apocrypha," and "Afterword," the last-named the opening poem of *Metropolitan Icons*. In more recent books Pilinszky returns to the lyric subgenre of the dramatic monologue. In *Crater* he cultivates it to great effect in the title poem, as well as in the two concluding major poems presented in this selection, "Miss I. B." and "Sketch."

"Crater" is a bemusing memoir of an evidently hectic relationship with an unnamed friend:

> You get off and get on.
> I get on and get off.
> Cigarette. You're pacing. I'm pacing.
> We walk in the same spot; like a murderer,
> I tailgate you as you walk.
>
> It's bird twitter, the way
> you reproach me for my birth. (136; 197)

The poem is a dramatic monologue—and a letter, never sent. The friend is no friend; the speaker is apparently much upset. The report on purposeless or frustrated movement resonates with situations depicted in the fiction of Franz Kafka;[52] it is a portrayal of a psychic state. The speaker in the poem both shows and states how he feels, but only up to a point; then he seems to cut himself off, and the closing image is one of facial expressions. The "I," ever since that slighting remark, has been making big eyes—in private. The feeling conveyed is one of irreparable estrangement; there is "that ... something / that is not you any more" (lines 16-18).

Pilinszky has a range; "Miss I. B." is another, very different, monologue-letter, rare in the oeuvre in that the voice is not the poet's, but rather that of an assigned role. The speaking subject is manifestly a female convict, an inmate at a correctional facility not unlike the one the poet experienced in his youth:

> Send me a comb and canned goods.
> The old comb broke, in a word.
>
> Send shoes. Warm undies.
> Imagine, they call me Iron Ball.
> Three more years. The garden is lousy. (143; 199)

Contradicting herself, Miss I. B. goes on to say: "Tomorrow I am here for the last time" (line 10). She alludes to an unspeakable offense: "Crime is what we succeed in / removing the very trace of" (lines 16-17). Shades of Raskolnikov, doing just that, after his axe murders? Perhaps. Beyond the scenes, in both "Crater" and "Miss I. B.," the poet guards the secrets of both slighted consciousness and guilty conscience. Here too we encounter silence; even the dramatic monologue genre is no guarantee that all shall be spoken out.

Our concluding translation, "Sketch," is of a poem based, as already mentioned, on Pilinszky's experiences as a child:

> Strike me dead. Your moustache keeps on growing,
> while I have a memory or two
> to tell me the exact difference
> between natural body heat
> and the heat of love.
>
> Though I was only five,
> and the girl sixteen. (143; 201)

Two warmths know of each other without meeting; a myriad of communications take place between them. How is this possible? Through another heat—that of the love that moves the poet to explore a relationship that exists only in the mind. In "Sketch" there is but a step this side of the flesh from Dante's platonic reminiscence of Beatrice, whom he saw once or twice, but with whom he presumably never exchanged more than a greeting (*La Vita Nuova*). And the poet reminds us of the fragility of life, of what is past:

> Micsicsák wore a prison garment,
> I a frilled collar and a little velvet outfit.
> She perished; I'm perishing. (144; 201)

Note the silence that remains language, the laconism, the eloquence and dramatic power of the understatement. "Sketch" is a very fully realized work; its theme of love is as much fulfilled, within its own domain, as is that of *Ulysses*. The question does, of course, emerge once again, as Tüskés broached it in connection with reading "Four-Liner": What does our knowing of the circumstances of the poet's life contribute to our understanding of the text? The answer is, Not by any means nothing. It is true that if there were no biography behind the poem we would still appreciate the tragic immediacy and fragility of the vision per se. But neither does it harm our chances of understanding to be aware of the external facts. We must at all times be mindful that Pilinszky, although capable of a great reserve of silence, understatement, and hermeticist compression and depth, is not ultimately a self-effacing poet. His numerous dedications alone enable us, just about, to trace his career, and of the powerful biographical relevance of the Holocaust poetry, which extends all the way to the poem "Auschwitz" (*Crater*), we have already spoken. This late piece, not so incidentally, once again tellingly contains the image of the five-year-old; compare with it the much earlier "Self-Portrait from 1944": "In the cold axis of his weeping / stands the boy" (*Metropolitan Icons*; *CP* 73). The boy is the adult Pilinszky, cast out of the Eden of his childish illusions by the horrendous reality of a world gone insane.

János Pilinszky is a poet of a curious blend of presences and absences, of which the eloquent silence of his minimalist and surrealist mode is but an ever-present aspect. Lacking in his poetry are said to be: redeemability, faith, directness, spontaneity, a strictly defined *ars poetica*, nature;[53] present is a lexicon that defines that pressure of absence: abstractions (the irreparable, the unacceptable, the unbearable, the unsayable, things of which we neither can nor may speak); Biblical imagery; images of corridor, eye, gallows smelling of bacon and geraniums, glass, hand, monstrance; the moon as a single, enormous blow; wrinkles in a face, on the back of a hand. It is a question of wilful limitation, of attending to instruments of our Passion, as it were. And the poet, in extremis, sticks at little or nothing. There are the images of hunger, and of the total surrender of our higher nature to the lower ("Frankfurt"), suggestions of cannibalism ("Paraphrase"), even of autophagy ("French Prisoner"). Indeed in wartime this poet went through and saw as much as anyone who survived, and the characteristic vocabulary of the poems is there to let us know that. But it does more. Never forgetting his privileged getaway, the poet forges in the smithy of his soul a terrible arsenal of poetic iron, words and lines and poems that taste like metals on the tongue. These are the sign systems of an intelligence that is at all times aware of its own doomed nature. As in "Straight Labyrinth" Pilinszky records what he knows of plunging, so too in the slightly earlier "Milyen felemás" ("[Among] What Assorted," not translated here) the poet sings: "we're plunging like a stone, / straight, and unambiguously" (lines 3-4; *CP* 106).

The poet, the "reporter" ("scribe") of "Admonition" is in the field to cover what alone is worth his while reporting. He instructs us in hard facts of a poetry which, as suggested above, is not designed to make us feel comfortable; which transports us, rather, to the country of last things. And yet, should there be occasion for umbrage at this unrelenting reminder that the universe and the soul have an underside, that indeed we are doomed, Pilinszky's vision is also saved. We recognize in this sensibility a reserve of kindness, of religiously attuned benignity. There can be no question that beyond the initial agnosticism, the wrestling with the divine ultimate he often does not seem sure is there at all, there is in Pilinszky's argument a recognizable measure of serene faith. It is not last a species of faith that the crucifixion of humanity that we have witnessed in our time brings us closer to understanding the crucifixion that for a believer of Pilinszky's stamp is our final hope. Along with Pilinszky's "agnostic faith" and identification with children comes ultimately also a sense of belonging: of adulthood, and a love of country, along with a great sympathy with that larger patriotism, toward "our homeland, Europe."[54] This too is a highly timely feeling.

We began by agreeing with Ágnes Nemes Nagy that Pilinszky is different. He is. Very different. And it benefits us to see just how different he is, as it benefits Hungarian and European poetry to have such "different" poets in their midst. But it would be a mistake to equate this difference either with a kind of irremediable simplicity and one-dimensionality, or with lack of comparability. To speak to the former danger, we see that Pilinszky's art is complex in the extreme. That this complexity is observable in part in the unexpected changes that his poetry undergoes over the years, and from book to book, we have noted. Complexity resides, in addition, in aspects of the language of poetry, of style, that are just beginning to be explored. The polysemy and multivalence of the individual word and phrase, of the relation between the word and the silence around it, between said and unsaid, the word chosen and the one left implied, are aspects of this complexity. In addition there is a burden of psychological complexity in the poet's insistent realization that, in the words of James Joyce, he is looking at "mortal beauty." Beauty and the moment privileged to record the encounter or nonencounter with it are mortal immanently and in transcendence both; in the helplessness of the poetic eye in meeting it and in then having to let it go, as with a sense that encounter and the desire to hold onto the moment of contemplated wonder are aspects of sin.[55] The atonement comes in the moment of letting go, in accepting the unalterable nature of the poetic here and now as being of a realm in which every moment of revelation draws with it a spiritual black hole of imploded truth, a truth to which we have no access. It is the way the gods work, and poets, real poets like Pilinszky, accept this structure of succession as a condition of their being poets at all. Of Pilinszky's order of acceptance are Celan, Dante, Hölderlin, Kafka, the most difficult writers, "those who have been there and back."[56]

This brings us to the question of Pilinszky's comparability, not last of his own consciousness of comparability. The poet of paradoxes, the recluse who was not one, the increasingly laconic poet capable of great dramatic monologues, of recitatives and plays; the Holocaust poet who disagreed with Theodor W. Adorno's dictum that it is not possible to write poetry after Auschwitz; finally the somber, saintly soul who was also able to socialize, to relax, and to smile-- all these personae of Pilinszky belong to a man and artist who knew: he belongs in the great company of European poets; he is different, but does not, for that, stand apart.[57] On the international scene, the roster of his fellow Holocaust poets would be a long one, but there are surprises, as yet unacknowledged presences, as well. Much has been made of W. H. Auden's statement, in his poem "In Memory of W. B. Yeats," that "poetry makes nothing happen." It may seem a puzzling pronouncement until we realize that "Auden has bluntly said that no poem of his, or of another, saved even one Jewish victim of the death camps."[58] With this, Pilinszky would agree. Yet he also knew that poetry is of such power and privileged status that it can make a great deal happen: it can bring home the horrors man perpetrates on his fellow humans, searing onto the screen of memory both the event and the blueprint of its vehicle. Fellow artists who saw as he did, and whose art underwent comparable transformations include, urgently, Paul Celan, the Celan both of "Death Fugue" and of the last minimalist poems.[59] And let me not leave unmentioned, among fellow poets of Pilinszky's own literature, Miklós Radnóti. Like Radnóti, Pilinszky went through and saw all that he recorded, and it makes little difference that in Radnóti's case we are talking about the military labor service, whereas Pilinszky's encounter was with death camps. One elemental fact that unites them is that neither experienced Auschwitz, although both were touched by it. Radnóti's stepmother and half sister both perished there.[60] Well after the camp had become a state museum, Pilinszky visited it with his sister, and wrote about it in eloquent prose. In the end the complexity, the paradoxical status of both poetry and poet may well mean that both Pilinszky and Nemes Nagy are right. The artist cannot and does not stand alone; the existentialist visionary and thinker also chooses for us. At the same time, Pilinszky's stature and moral stance ultimately place him where any poet of his rank belongs—in a class by himself.

III

I have been translating the poems of János Pilinszky, and submitting my versions to magazines, since approximately the fall of 1977. I am grateful for the success that these translations have had. About one half of the seventy-two included in this selection have found their way into magazines and anthologies, some of the best poetry forums in North America, as noted in the Acknowledgments.

The secret of Pilinszky's success in English is not difficult to guess. His different directness, minimalism, sudden silences and frustrated motions all point to dream syntax, and to the kind of dry, tough poetry that has long been in favor with modernists, avantgardistes, and postmodernists in the United States and in Canada. His translatability is another matter. He would seem to be relatively easy to translate; certainly he does not pose the challenges of a hexametrist like Radnóti, or of such a folk-song artist and linguist as Weöres. But this kind of ease and relative simplicity can be very deceptive. I promise the reader that it took a great deal of thought, revision, and filing to arrive at these American versions. I stress their Americanness because the two principal previous translations I know, those of Hughes and Csokits and Peter Jay, are British. I do not wish to say anything negative about either. They both had their eloquent justification in their time; and Pilinszky himself rejoiced in their appearance.[61] They also both have their merits. But it is equally true that if the poet is different, then his translator had better try to be different also. The present offering is, I hope, a Pilinszky with an audibly new voice, a poet in English who has not been heard before. Above all I trust that I have succeeded in giving every line its due weight, in letting the poem, either in its full eloquence or in its bone-bare laconism, settle with the weight of words carefully chosen, the translations written as if they were original English poems. This does, of course, bear implications for manner and style; this translator, a poet in his own right, cannot help adding his voice to that of the translated poet. Once again I translated solo, directly off the Hungarian page.[62]

A translator's responsibility is to his poet. I hope I have succeeded in capturing the important qualities and the atmosphere of this poetry, of the poet, and of the man without whom there is no poet. I wanted the unpretentiousness to come across, but also the craft, the sheer courage, for example, of making some of the Holocaust poetry in a passionately rhymed and metered medium. Once again I have tried, as I did in my work on Radnóti's poetry, to be faithful to the form and total sound of a poem, not because Pilinszky cared much about the translator's art, which he arguably did not,[63] but because I wanted to show the reader without access to the originals precisely what kind of poet Pilinszky was. Despite its noted monumentality and iconicity, Pilinszky's poetry is quintessentially not a poetry of monoliths; it is a poetry of spiritual becoming, of striving. He did not consider himself to be a poet, but said he felt the need to write when he did, when he felt compelled to "make his move."[64] But this also means that the power of the individual word may be more important to him than the formal equipoise of a text. This too is why I felt that on occasion it was wiser to let a rhyme go, or to take the hint from the poet and to work with off-rhymes, a device with which Pilinszky shows great skill. Some of Pilinszky's most successful poems, of course, are those that do not rhyme at all (e.g., "For Jutta," "Through a Lifetime," "Spaces," "Gothic," "Crater").

A word about the selection itself. As the table of contents shows, I have tried to account for each of the six major books and for their central concerns as fully as is permitted by a selection of seventy-two poems, about one-third of Pilinszky's total output. All seventy-two texts are in verse; I have not touched the three prose poems in *Dénouement*. I have translated none of the uncollected verse, nor have I considered any of the verse tales, the latter charming and valid in themselves, but not a part of the Pilinszky canon in the present sense. I did try to include very nearly all of the Holocaust poetry, not last "KZ Oratorio," as well as some of the important surrealist and minimalist verse, especially in the last two collections. Several of the inscribed poems are here; the relation of poem to dedicatee at times presents fascinating problems. Above all, I hope that this bilingual volume does justice to a great artist within the limits of an initial selection. The present book tries to acquaint the interested reader with a major poet who may well be more "different" to Hungarian ears than he is to American ones at home with our most important minimalist voices. Let me also hope that the offering, timely as it is in the area of poetics, is no less so as an act of bearing witness for our time, as Pilinszky has bravely borne witness for his.

A note on the Hungarian text: It is diplomatic, after the 1987 *Collected Poems*, and accounts scrupulously for the poet's often seemingly idiosyncratic notions concerning vowel length. As the editor, István Jelenits, notes in his Afterword (*CP* 230), more often than not Pilinszky's grounds for deviating from standard orthographic practice are prosodic.

NOTES

In these notes and in the Notes on the Poems, sources cited in abbreviated form will be found listed in the Bibliography.

1. See Miklós Radnóti, *Subway Stops: Fifty Poems*, ed. and trans. Emery George, Ardis World Poets in Translation series, 4 (Ann Arbor: Ardis, 1977). Since then have appeared: Miklós Radnóti, *The Complete Poetry*, ed. and trans. Emery George (Ann Arbor: Ardis, 1980) (cited as *MR* and page); and Emery George, *The Poetry of Miklós Radnóti: A Comparative Study* (New York: Karz-Cohl, 1986) (cited as *PMR* and page).

2. See Ágnes Nemes Nagy, "Ekhnáton éjszakája" ("Ikhnaton's Night"), from *A lovak és az angyalok: Válogatott versek* (The Horses and the Angels: Selected Poems) (1969), as in: Á. N. N., *Között: Összegyűjtött versek* (Between: Collected Poems) (Budapest: Magvető, 1981) 152-54. For an English translation, by Laura Schiff, see *Contemporary East European Poetry: An Anthology*, ed. Emery George (New York, Oxford: Oxford UP, 1993) 261-63.

3. Nemes Nagy, 1981, 58.

4. Nemes Nagy, 1981, 54.

5. See Tüskés 15. To date this is the only biography of János Pilinszky available.

6. Tüskés 17-19 (operatic tenors), 19, 44-46 (father), 19-21 (mother's family origins), 24-26 (Bébi), 26-32 (institution for delinquent girls), 32 (stress on role of eye). On JP's musician uncles, see also *Convv.* 182-83.

7. Tüskés 34-37 (elementary schooling), 37-38 (secondary education), 37-41 (teachers), 41 (Pilinszky's grades, interest in sports), 41, 47-48 (literary interests and student circle), 41-44 (readings), 48 (matters of importance to JP as poet). On 48 Tüskés quotes a radio interview with Éva Tóth titled "A világ peremén" ("On the World's Edge"); see *Convv.* 149-55; 150.

8. Tüskés 21-24 (on appearance of "Anyám" ["My Mother"], with text). For text, see also *CP* 147.

9. Tüskés 61-77, 90-94, 99-118 (collaboration with literary magazines), 59 (university graduation), 59, 88 (dissertation burned in siege of Budapest).

10. Tüskés 78-89 (JP's call-up and war experiences), 85 (JP's reply to

interviewer's question). Cf. explicit denial: "Were you a prisoner, too?" "I was not." See László Cs. Szabó, "Aljosa: Első beszélgetés Pilinszky Jánossal" ("Alyosha: First Conversation with J. P."), *Convv.* 10-24; 16.

11. Tüskés 82. With the exception of "On the Third Day," the poems whose titles are cited in text immediately preceding the quotation are all translated in this selection and are for the most part also quoted in part 2 of this Introduction. For the form of citation in this essay of both the Hungarian source and the present selection, see below, n. 29.

12. János Pilinszky, "Ars poetica helyett" ("Instead of an *ars poetica*"), from the collection *Metropolitan Icons* (1970), as in *CP* 80-83; 80-81. On "models," see Tüskés 85.

13. An idea of Simone Weil's importance for JP may be obtained by consulting the index to *Nadir* (2:230, with no fewer than thirty-nine entries). On Weil, see also Tüskés 195-98 (with portrait, 194), and the note on "For Jutta" (in the Notes on the Poems, to rear of volume).

14. Tüskés 85; on JP's dating of his poems, Tüskés 145.

15. Tüskés 93-97; see especially discussion of reviews, Tüskés 96-97.

16. See JP, in "Alyosha," first interview with Cs. Szabó, *Convv.* 22.

17. See JP's own statement, *Convv.* 25. On the officially silenced years, see also Tüskés 116-20.

18. Tüskés 165.

19. For full citation of independent book publications (poetry collections, verse tales, occasional prose, interviews), see the Bibliography. All other writings here referred to form parts of books as follows: the verse translations (from Hugo von Hofmannsthal, Heinrich Heine, Robert Burns, and Pierre Emmanuel) will be found in *CP* 211-27; the four minimalist plays: *Gyerekek és katonák* (Children and Soldiers), *Síremlék* (Grave Monument), *"Urbi et Orbi"* – *A testi szenvedésről* ("Urbi et Orbi"—On Physical Suffering), and *Élőképek* (Tableaux Vivants), in *Dénouement* 51-119 (also in *Nadir* 2:51-119); the film script *Rekviem* (Requiem), in the collection titled *Rekviem* 39-104; *Beszélgetések Sheryl Suttonnal: Egy párbeszéd regénye* (Conversations with Sheryl Sutton: The Novel of a Dialogue), in *Nadir* 2:121-89. For this last entry, see also the English translation, published as an independent book. On the verse tales and plays, see S. Radnóti, 1974.

20. Tüskés 193 (Emmanuel), 195-98 (Weil).

21. See Tüskés 300-02 (chronology), 241-42 (Marcel), 199-201 (Switzerland, including photo of Dürrenmatt, 198), 199 (Poland). See also JP's articles "Varsói képeslap" ("Postcard from Warsaw"), "Krakkó" ("Cracow"), "Czenstochowa," and "Oswiecim" (*Nadir* 1:263-70); also "Három találkozás" ("Three Encounters"), with the subheadings "Paul Klee," "Dürrenmatt," and "Valsainte" (*Nadir* 1:295-97). For the text of the poem "Gyónás után" ("After Confession"), see 124; 171.

22. Tüskés 202-06 (on Poetry International and Anglophone poets, including Ted Hughes), 246-48 (on appearance of 1976 *Selected Poems*, with reproduction of title page, 247). See also the interview with Cs. Szabó "Versünk a világban: Második beszélgetés Pilinszky Jánossal" ("Our Poem in the World: Second Conversation with J. P."), *Convv.* 44-70; also Csokits, 1992, 94-109, 121-24 (letters).

23. Tüskés 205 (JP on sound recordings as a way of preserving his work).

24. Tüskés 246.

25. Tüskés 266 (with sleeve of recording reproduced, 265). I have not heard the recording, but have examined the score: György Kurtág, *Négy dal Pilinszky János verseire* / ... / *Four Songs to Poems by János Pilinszky*, op. 11, UE 16841 (Vienna: Universal Edition; Budapest: Editio Musica, 1979). Thanks are due to the Music Library, Columbia University.

26. See, among others, the cover of *Convv.* and the inside back cover of Tüskés, the latter showing the poet presumably at the time of his receipt of the Kossuth Prize.

27. Tüskés 154-57, 267-69 (helpfulness, interviews), 154, 281-82 (concern about his health), 287 (receives Kossuth Prize), 288-91 (death and burial).

28. Tüskés 6.

29. Following set-off quotations, as here, as well as in text, the first page number appearing in parentheses cites *CP*; the second, this selection (English text only). This form of citation also applies to these notes, and to the Notes on the Poems. Poems cited by *CP* and page only are not translated in the present selection.

30. On Pilinszky's iambs, see Görgey; also S. Radnóti 117-19.

31. Tüskés 94 (on the repositioning of "Harbach 1944"). All six of JP's poetry collections are organized in cycles; see only the table of contents of *CP* (243-52). The title *On the Third Day* could as well have been *Tertia die*, the

wording of the closing line of the poem "On the Third Day" being "Et resurrexit tertia die" (*CP* 42). I left the title in English, reasoning that if it were to have been in Latin, JP could have made that decision, too. *Harmadnapon* (On the Third Day) appeared in September of 1959 (Tüskés 147).

32. 27-28; 13, *CP* 29-30. 30-31; 17, 31; 19. *CP* 32-33, *CP* 33-34. This last-named poem is inscribed to the distinguished sculptor Béni Ferenczy (1890-1967), who executed a terracotta bust of JP in 1954; see Tüskés 129 (reproduction of bust), 131 (photo of artist). See also JP's three articles on BF in *Nadir* (1:191-92, 233, 513-14), as well as György Rónay's diary entry for 9 September 1952, in which he alludes to a visit, in the company of JP, to Ferenczy's studio (Rónay, *Diaries*, 1:621-22).

33. *CP* 15-16 ("On a Forbidden Star"), *CP* 36-38 ("In No Man's Land"). On the latter, see Tandori, 1980.

34. See Tüskés 169 (characteristic lexicon); S. Radnóti 119-20 (on JP's "inner system of reference"); Tandori, 1983.

35. 39-40; 21, 23. 40-41; 25, 27. 41-42; 29. 42; 31. *CP* 42. 43-44; 33, 35, 37. 48-50; 47, 49, 51, 53. (In the citations in this note, as in n. 32, period dots indicate what belongs together.)

36. See Anthony Hecht, *The Hard Hours* (New York: Atheneum, 1967) 39 (poem "The Room," in the cycle *Rites and Ceremonies*). Hecht's achievement in Holocaust poetry invites comparison with JP's. JP mentions Hecht as a fellow participant in the 1969 Poets' Biennale, London (*Convv.* 33), where they presumably met.

37. As quoted in the article "Oswiecim," *Nadir* 1:268-70; 269. The literature on ES is considerable; see only Waltraud Herbstrith, *Edith Stein: A Biography*, trans. Father Bernard Bonowitz, OCSO (San Francisco, New York: Harper & Row, 1985); and Reiner Wimmer, *Vier jüdische Philosophinnen: Rosa Luxemburg, Simone Weil, Edith Stein, Hannah Arendt* (Tübingen: Attempto, 1990) 169-236.

38. In its first publication, in *Új Írás* (New Writing) 2, no. 12 (December 1962): 1365-72; see also the main title and subtitle of "KZ Oratorio," the collection *Requiem* 105. The phrase "My dark heaven" is spoken by the young girl, M. R., toward the end of the play, just before the overhead lights go out (67; 91). On "KZ Oratorio," see also *Convv.* 16-19.

39. Tüskés 173. Far more acceptable is the comment on "KZ Oratorio" in

xlix

Fülöp 184-86. In the contexts of both "KZ Oratorio" and the film script *Requiem*, see also JP's "Háborús Requiem" ("War Requiem") (*Nadir* 1:316-18), reviewing a performance of Benjamin Britten's work. The review dates from 25 December 1966.

40. A condition of his art of which JP himself was keenly aware. See only his statement, in the first interview with Cs. Szabó, that he, JP, feels closer to the immobility of Byzantine icon painting than to the ever increasing dynamism of Western painting since the trecento (*Convv.* 14).

41. See Tüskés 176-79 (Dostoyevsky), 194-98 (Weil), 179 (Van Gogh), 248-55 (J. S. Bach and music); also *Nadir* 2:226, 230, 230, 225 (index entries, respectively). On Bach, see also *Convv.* 156-57, 183, 186.

42. Tüskés 165-68, Fülöp 175-81. See also the concluding paragraph of JP's essay "Instead of an *ars poetica*" (*CP* 83). George Steiner, in his essay "Silence and the Poet," writes of the larger context; see G. S., *Language and Silence: Essays on Language, Literature, and the Inhuman* (New York: Atheneum, 1967) 36-54; 46-54. Steiner discusses silence in, among others, Hölderlin, Rilke, and Kafka. Steiner, Susan Sontag, and Theodor W. Adorno, all three on silence, are also cited in Fülöp, n. 74 (242).

43. Tüskés 165. Cf. above, n. 18.

44. They are: "A tengerpartra" ("On the Seashore"), "Ama kései" ("That Belated"), "Négysoros" ("Four-Liner"), "Agonia Christiana," "A harmadik" ("The Third"), "Hideg szél" ("Cold Wind") (*CP* 28, 38, 51, 51, 52, 52). Only "Four-Liner" is included in our selection.

45. Tüskés 128-34. See also Kuklay 123-28; Nemes Nagy, 1988; Tamás; and the detailed citations in Fülöp, n. 55 (241).

46. Tüskés 130.

47. Unlike Tüskés (134), who nevertheless is cautious, or Kuklay (123) who, without comment, quotes and cites biographical material.

48. See Pomogáts 143; also Vas.

49. See the note on "Metropolitan Icons" in the Notes on the Poems. More on Magrittean effects in the notes on "To Two Lovers" and "The Henchman's Room."

50. See Delmore Schwartz, "Summer Knowledge," in: D. S., *Selected Poems 1938-1958: Summer Knowledge* (New York: New Directions, pbk., 1967) 157-58. Robert Wilson's play *Deafman Glance* is itself about death and

rebirth and new "summer knowledge"; see the note on "Crime and Punishment." 51. For the text of Hölderlin's poem, see Hanser 1:445 (this edition is fully cited in the note on "Under a Winter Sky"). The images of the close of "Hälfte des Lebens" are echoed also in the silences of JP's poem "Hölderlin" (134; 189).

52. I cannot agree with Kuklay that the person addressed is a woman; on this, see the note on "Crater." On frustrated movement in the poetry, see Béládi 462; on Kafka, see below, n. 56.

53. See Béládi 457 (irredeemability); Béládi 460, Pálmai 582 (lack of faith); Domonkos and Valaczka (lack of directness); Diószegi 1676 (lack of spontaneity); Koppány and Kocsis 53 (lack of a strictly defined *ars poetica*); Pomogáts 143 (lack of nature; on this, see also above, n. 48). See also Lengyel.

54. There can be no question that JP, who had a special liking for traveling, would have positive feelings for "our homeland, Europe"; on "love of country," see *Convv.* 135-36, 194-95 (the latter on Simone Weil's recommendation on the subject, instigated by her reading of Homer).

55. See especially the poem "Bűn" ("Sin") (*CP* 29-30) and "Rongyaidban és kitakarva" ("In Your Rags and Uncovered") (*CP* 97); also entries on subject area of "sin" (*Nadir* 2:231); not listed there: "Három etűd a bűnről" ("Three Etudes on Sin") (*Nadir* 2:212-20).

56. On Paul Celan, "of whom I dare not state that he is a greater poet than Rilke," see *Convv.* 212 (also 65); on Hölderlin, see especially the notes on "Apocrypha" and "Hölderlin"; on Franz Kafka, see *Nadir* 2:227, especially *Nadir* 1:398-99.

57. See the interview with Mátyás Domokos, "A költői jelenlét" ("Poetic Presence"), *Convv.* 91-110. On "presence," see also the poem "Noon."

58. See Edward Callan, *Auden: A Carnival of Intellect* (New York, Oxford: Oxford UP, 1983) 150. This is confirmed, with reference to Auden's 1939 decision to withdraw from politics, in Humphrey Carpenter, *W. H. Auden: A Biography* (Boston: Houghton Mifflin, 1981) 255-57 (the line "For poetry makes nothing happen" discussed, 256).

59. See the article by Wirth, a limited study of affinities rather than of specific points of intersection. On Celan, see also above, n. 56. For representative samples of the work of other poets of Pilinszky's capability, see the anthology *Against Forgetting: Twentieth-Century Poetry of Witness*, ed. Carolyn Forché (New York: Norton, 1993).

60. On the fates of Miklós Radnóti's stepmother and half sister, see *PMR* 651 (chap. 13, n. 33); also *MR* 391. That MR and JP are the only two Hungarian Holocaust poets of consequence is discussed also in Sanders 193-96.

61. See Csokits 1992; also Tüskés 246-48 (with reproduction of title page, 247). See also above, n. 22.

62. On the principles of solo translation, see my article "Translating Poetry: Notes on a Solitary Craft," *The Kenyon Review* 4, no. 2 (Spring 1982): 33-54.

63. See only JP's second interview with Cs. Szabó, *Convv.* 44-70, where exploration of the problems of translating poetry is almost totally lacking.

64. Chess metaphor; see *Convv.* 22 ("I make the move when I must").

METROPOLITAN ICONS

SELECTED POEMS OF JÁNOS PILINSZKY

from *Trapeze and Parallel Bars* (1946)

TÉLI ÉG ALATT

Cholnoky Tamásnak

Fejem fölé a csillagok
jeges tüzet kavarnak,
az irgalmatlan ég alatt
hanyattdölök a falnak.

A szomorúság tétován
kicsordul árva számon.
Mivé is lett az anyatej?
Beszennyezem kabátom.

Akár a kő, olyan vagyok,
mindegy mi jön, csak jöjjön.
Oly engedelmes, jó leszek,
végig esem a földön.

Tovább nem ámitom magam,
nincsen ki megsegítsen,
nem vált meg semmi szenvedés,
nem véd meg semmi isten.

Ennél már semmi nem lehet
se egyszerűbb, se szörnyebb:
lassan megindulnak felém
a bibliai szörnyek.

UNDER A WINTER SKY

For Tamás Cholnoky

Over my head the stars
mix icy fire;
under the merciless sky I lean
supine against the wall.

Hesitant, sadness
runs from my orphan mouth.
What has mother milk become?
I'm soiling my topcoat.

I am just like a stone;
whatever comes, let it come.
I'll be so obedient, so good,
I'll slam flat on the ground.

I'll deceive myself no longer:
there's no one around to help me,
no suffering will redeem,
no god will protect me.

Nothing could be simpler
than this, nothing more monstrous.
Slowly they start out toward me:
the biblical monsters.

KÉSŐ KEGYELEM

Mit kezdjen, akit elitélt,
de fölmentett később az ég,
megvonva tőle a halált,
mikor már megadta magát?

Kit mindenétől üresen
talált a szörnyű kegyelem,
megsemmisülten, mielőtt
a semmi habjaiba dőlt!

Mit kezdjen itt! Közületek
talányait ki fejti meg?
Szorongva anyját kémleli:
ha elzokoghatná neki!

Fogódzanék akárkibe,
de nem lesz soha senkije;
szeméből, mint gazdátlan ág,
kicsüng a pusztuló világ.

BELATED GRACE

What should he do: the one heaven
condemned, but later acquitted,
depriving him of death
once he had surrendered?

One whom horrible grace
found emptied of all he possessed,
annihilated, before he toppled
into the surf of nothingness?

What is he to do here! Among you,
who will solve his riddles?
Anguished, he spies his mother:
could he but weep them to her!

Whomever he may hang onto,
never will he have a soul;
from his eye, like an ownerless branch,
hangs a perishing world.

MERT ÁZTATOK ÉS FÁZTATOK

Rónay Györgynek

Forduljatok hát ellenem
ti meglapuló szörnyek,
az omló folyosókon át
hatolva egyre följebb,
nyomuljatok be szabadon,
futótüzet kiáltva
lassan fölétek rakodó
hatalmas éjszakámba!

Csupaszra vetkőztessetek,
semmit se hagyva rajtam,
vegyétek el a homlokom,
a szemem és az ajkam,
mert áztatok és fáztatok,
mert éheztetek bennem,
bár én is áztam-fáztam és
nekem se volt mit ennem.

Legyűrhetetlen fölkelés,
dadogó, győztes lárma!
mint életfogytig elitélt
fegyencek lázadása.
Egyetlen boldog pillanat,
a végső és az első:
csak állok majd és reszketek,
akár egy égő erdő.

BECAUSE YOU WERE SOAKING WET, WERE COLD

For György Rónay

Turn, then, against me,
you monsters lying in wait,
advancing through the crumbling
corridors, ever higher;
press on freely, crowd in,
raising the alarm of wildfire,
into my enormous night
slowly piling on top of you!

Strip me to the bare skin,
leaving on me nothing;
take from me my brow,
my eyes, and my lips,
because you were soaking wet, were cold,
because in me you knew hunger,
though I was soaked and cold myself,
and had nothing to eat, either.

Mutiny not to be quelled,
stammering noise—triumph!
like a rebellion of convicts
sentenced to life.
A single happy moment,
the last and the first:
I'll just stand and tremble,
like a burning forest.

from *On the Third Day* (1959)

PARAFRÁZIS

Mindenki táplálékaként,
ahogy már írva van,
adom, mint élő eledelt,
a világnak magam.

Mert minden élő egyedűl
az elevenre éhes,
lehet a legjobb szeretőd,
végül is összevérez.

Csak hányódom hát ágyamon
és beléreszketek,
hogy kikkel is zabáltatom
a szívverésemet!

Miféle vályu ez az ágy,
ugyan miféle vályú?
S mi odalök, micsoda vágy,
tündöklő tisztaságú!

Szünetlen érkező szivem
hogy falja föl a horda!
Eleven táplálék vagyok
dadogva és dobogva.

Eleven étketek vagyok
szünetlen és egészen;
emésszétek föl lényegem,
hogy éhségtek megértsem.

PARAPHRASE

For everyone's nourishment
—as it's now on record—
I give myself to the world
as living food.

For all that lives hungers
after the living alone,
be it your best lover, in the end
she'll cover you with gore.

So I toss on my bed
and tremble at the thought
of just who it is I'm feeding
my heartbeat!

What sort of trough is this bed,
yes, what kind of feeder?
And what gleaming, clean longing
thrusts me there!

Heart ceaselessly arriving:
how the horde chomps it!
I'm living nourishment,
stammering, stomping.

I am your live sustenance,
without pause, the whole;
that I may grasp your hunger—
digest my soul.

Mert aki végkép senkié,
az mindenki falatja.
Pusztíts hát szörnyű szerelem.
Ölj meg. Ne hagyj magamra.

For whoever in the end is no one's,
is everyone's morsel.
Destroy me, then, terrible love.
Kill me. Don't leave me to myself.

TANUK NÉLKÜL

Kirajzolódom végleg a világból,
mint csupasz falnak állitott fogoly,
külön kezel, kivételes magányban
a tanuk nélkül dolgozó pokol.

Egy porcikám se bízná senki másra,
ha únja már, magam kezére ad,
s én folytatom, hol éppen abbahagyta,
a két kezemmel, úgy és ugyanazt.

Ki itt találna rám e szörnyüségben,
és végignézné, mit is művelek,
nem hinné el tulajdon két szemének,
s egy szót se merne szólni senkinek.

Íly nyomorúság ugyan mire várna?
Mi hátra van, bevégzi egymaga,
hogy holta után is beléremeg,
meg-megrándul a hóhér kosara.

WITHOUT WITNESSES

With finality I am outlined against the world,
like a prisoner stood against a bare wall;
hell, working without witnesses, treats me
in exceptional solitude, with special protocol.

No particle of me would it entrust
to anyone else; when weary, it hands me over
to myself, and I take it from where it stopped,
with my two hands, its way, the same as ever.

Whoever should find me in this horror,
and look on at just what I have done,
he would not believe his own two eyes,
nor dare breathe a word to anyone.

Just what is it such misery might wait for?
What is left he'll finish, and no mistake.
So that even after his death, the henchman's
basket will twitch off and on, will shake.

KÉT SZERETŐRE

Mint alvilági házasok
a forró sodronyon,
hevertek, mint a balfelem,
balom a jobbomon,
s bár oktalan szerelmetek
már annyit sem jelent,
mint illemhely sivár falán
az ábrák és jelek:
a tűrhetetlen megszokás
megannyi változat
és változás között vakon
mégiscsak összetart!
Akár a kettészelt kukac
valahogy mégis egy,
szived szivével esztelen
vesződve hempereg!

Bizony: a büntetés elől
kár is lesz futnotok,
egy óriási csecsemő
állja el utatok,
és hanyatt-homlok menekül
a torkotokon át,
véres csomóban kiszakad,
megszökik a világ.

TO TWO LOVERS

Like married couples of the underworld
on the hot spun cable
as my left half you lie,
on my right, my left;
and though your mindless love means
not even so much any more
as graffiti and signs
on a bleak outhouse wall,
intolerable habit is
so much variety
and, blindly, in all that change,
holds its integrity!
Just as an earthworm, sliced
in two, is yet somehow one,
so, mindlessly, your heart
wrestles with his, rumples on!

Oh yes—it's hardly any use
fleeing your punishment:
blocking your escape route
is an enormous infant,
and there, in headlong flight,
through and out your throats,
breaking free, the world
escapes, in bloodfilled clots.

HARBACH 1944

Thurzó Gábornak

Újra és újra őket látom,
a hold süt és egy rúd mered,
s a rúd elé emberek fogva
húznak egy roppant szekeret.

Vonják a növő éjszakával
növekvő óriás kocsit,
a testükön a por, az éhség
és reszketésük osztozik.

Viszik az utat és a tájat,
a fázó krumpliföldeket,
de mindennek csak súlyát érzik,
a tájakból a terheket.

Csak szomszédjuk esendő testét,
mely szinte beléjük tapad,
amint eleven rétegekben
egymás nyomában inganak.

A falvak kitérnek előlük
és félre állnak a kapuk,
elébük jött a messzeség és
megtántorodva visszafut.

Térdig gázolnak botladozva
facipőiknek alacsony,
sötéten zörrenő zajában,
mint láthatatlan avaron.

HARBACH 1944

For Gábor Thurzó

Again and again I see them:
bright moon and a shaft, hard,
and, harnessed to the shaft, men
pull an enormous cart.

They pull the gigantic cart,
which grows with the growing night;
from their bodies dust, hunger,
and their trembling take a bite.

They haul the road, the land,
the shivering potato fields;
but of all it's only the weight,
the lands' burden they feel.

Only their neighbor's frail body,
which all but sticks to them,
as in living layers they totter
in one another's footsteps.

The villages step aside,
and aside, the manor gates;
distance has met them, runs,
staggering, back apace.

To their knees they wade, stumbling
in their wooden shoes' shallow
darkly clattering noise,
as on invisible fallen leaves.

De törzsük már a némaságé.
Magasba mártják arcukat,
feszülten mintha szimatolnák
a messze égi vályukat.

Mert fogadásukra már készen,
akár egy megnyiló karám,
kapuit vadul széttaszítva
sarkig kitárult a halál.

But muteness has their torsoes now.
They dip their faces aloft,
tensely, as if they sniffed
heaven's faraway troughs.

For, ready now to receive them,
like some opening pen,
wildly, its gates to the hinges,
death has flung itself open.

FRANCIA FOGOLY

Csak azt feledném, azt a franciát, kit
hajnalfele a szállásunk előtt
a hátsó udvar sűrüjében láttam
lopódzani, hogy szinte földbe nőtt.
Körülkutatva éppen visszanézett,
s hogy végre biztos rejteket talált:
övé lehet a zsákmánya egészen!
Akármi lesz is, nem mozdul odább.

S már ette is, már falta is a répát,
mit úgy lophatott rongyai alatt.
Nyers marharépát evett, de a torkán
még alig ért le, jött is a falat;
és undorral és gyönyörrel a nyelvén
az édes étel úgy találkozott,
mint telhetetlen testi mámorukban
a boldogok és boldogtalanok!

Csak azt a testet, reszkető lapockát,
a csupa bőr és csupa csont kezet,
a tenyerét, mely úgy tapadt a szájra
es úgy adott, hogy maga is evett!
Az egymás ellen keserülő szervek
reménytelen és dühödt szégyenét,
amint a végső összetartozást is
önönmaguktól kell, hogy elvegyék!

FRENCH PRISONER

Could I but forget that one, the Frenchman
whom in front of our quarters, around dawn,
I saw in the thick of the back yard,
stealing, all but grown into the ground.
Searching around, he was just looking back
and, having found, secure at last, a lair:
his loot can be his, and all of it!
Come what may, he'll never move from there.

And he was eating, gorging on the turnip
he must have stolen, like that, under his rags.
He ate raw cattle turnip, but in his throat
hardly would it go down, but up it comes;
and on his tongue the sweet food met
with disgust and with the yen to enjoy it,
the way the happy and unhappy meet
in their bodies' insatiable delight!

If only that body, that trembling shoulder blade,
that hand, nothing but skin and all but bones,
that palm of his, which stuck to his mouth and fed
so that it itself ate of that morsel!
The hopeless and enraged humiliation
of organs embittered at one another,
as they must deprive their very selves
of their ultimate belonging together!

Az állatian makogó örömről
a suta lábát ahogy lemaradt,
és semmisülten kuporgott a testnek
vad gyönyöre és gyötrelme alatt!
A pillantását, – azt fcledném egyszer!
Ha fuldokolva is, de falt tovább,
és egyre még, és mindegy már akármit,
csak enni bármit, ezt-azt, önmagát!

Minek folytassam? – Őrök jöttek érte;
a szomszéd fogolytáborból szökött.
S én bolyongok, mint akkor is a kertben,
az itthoni kert árnyai között.
A jegyzetembe nézek és idézem:
"Csak azt fcledném, azt a franciát..."
S a fülemből, a szememből, a számból
a heves emlék forrón rámkiált:

"Éhes vagyok!" – És egyszeriben érzem
a halhatatlan éhséget, amit
a nyomorult már réges-rég nem érez,
se földi táplálék nem csillapít.
Belőlem él! És egyre éhesebben!
És egyre kevesebb vagyok neki!
Ki el lett volna bármi eleségen:
most már a szívemet követeli.

That ungainly foot of his, that beastly
jibbering-mumbling gladness that it missed
as, under the body's wild delight and torment,
annihilated it huddled, erased!
His glance—could I forget but that, just once!
Even if choking, he'd continue to wolf,
and on and on—what's the difference, what?
to eat, whatever, this or that, himself!

Why should I go on? Guards came to get him;
he had fled from the prison camp next door.
And I roam, as I did in the garden then,
among the shades of the garden here at home.
I glance into my notes and quote the line:
"Could I but forget that one, the Frenchman ... ."
And out my ears, my eyes, my mouth,
fiery memory yells at me, singeing:

"I'm hungry!" And suddenly I feel
the hunger that cannot and will not die,
which the wretch has not felt for so long,
and which no earthly food will satisfy.
He lives on me! And ever hungrier!
And for him I am ever the smaller part!
He, who would have survived on any food,
now returns to claim my very heart.

EGY KZ-LÁGER FALÁRA

Ahova estél, ott maradsz.
A mindenségből ezt az egyet,
ezt az egyetlen egy helyet,
de ezt azután megszerezted.

Menekül előled a táj.
Lehet az ház, malom vagy nyárfa,
minden csak küszködik veled,
mintha a semmiben mutálna.

De most már te nem tágitasz.
Megvakitottunk? Szemmel tartasz.
Kifosztottunk? Meggazdagodtál.
Némán, némán is reánkvallasz.

ON A KZ LAGER'S WALL

Where you fell, there you will remain.
Of the whole universe this one,
this single solitary place,
this, I daresay—you have made your own.

The land flees you.
Be it house, mill, or poplar,
all that things do is struggle with you,
as if their voices cracked in the void.

But no: you will not yield any more now.
Did we blind you? You hold us with your eyes.
Did we rob you? You have grown wealthy.
Mutely, even mutely, you testify against us.

RAVENSBRÜCKI PASSIÓ

Kilép a többiek közűl,
megáll a kockacsendben,
mint vetitett kép hunyorog
rabruha és fegyencfej.

Félelmetesen maga van,
a pórusait látni,
mindene olyan óriás,
mindene oly parányi.

És nincs tovább. A többi már,
a többi annyi volt csak,
elfelejtett kiáltani
mielőtt földre roskadt.

RAVENSBRÜCK PASSION

He steps out from among the rest,
stops in the cube silence;
like a projected picture, inmate
clothes and prisoner head blink.

He is fearfully alone;
you can see his pores,
all of him so gigantic,
all so minuscule.

And that is it. The rest,
the rest was merely
that he forgot to let out a shout
before falling down in a heap.

FRANKFURT

A folyóparton üres homokbánya,
oda hordtuk nyáron a szemetet.
Villák között és kertek közt suhantunk,
egy híd, egy lejtős út következett,
a lóversenytér deszkakerítése,
pár zökkenő, az autó lassitott,
de mielőtt még fékezhetett volna,
az első éhség máris támadott!

A tömött zsákok és kidöntött vödrök,
a helyezkedő hátak terrora,
a föltaszított ládák közt megindult
az előzetes, gyilkos cenzura;
osztozkodás a hulladék kövérjén,
hogy alig állta saját rohamát
a négykézlábra ereszkedett éhség,
és föllázadt, és megadta magát.

Belevesztek a porba és piszokba;
az egész kocsi bőgve reszketett,
a szivüket a moslék elkeverte
és összemosta eszméletüket.
A tele kannák mélyire kotorva,
hogy szemük-szájuk elborult vele,
belehaltak az eleven lucsokba,
es föltámadtak fejjel lefele.

FRANKFURT

On the riverbank an empty sand pit;
in summer, we would use it as a landfill.
Among villas and gardens we would scurry,
a bridge followed, a road downhill,
the plank-board fence of the race course;
a jolt or two, the car slowed down,
but even before it could brake,
the first hunger pangs attacked!

Terror of stuffed bags and capsized buckets,
of backs trying to get comfortable;
among the kicked-over crates, preemptive,
murderous censorship was underway;
sharing in the fat of kitchen leavings,
oh yes: forced onto all fours, hunger
could scarcely stand its very own onslaught—
and it rebelled, and straightaway surrendered.

They got lost among the grit and dirt;
the whole vehicle shook and wept;
hog slop blended away their hearts,
and washed away their consciousness.
Scraping to the bottoms of the full cans,
so that their eyes and mouths would all but drown,
they died of partaking of living swill,
and were resurrected upside down.

És visszavették, falatról-falatra,
mi velük együtt végképp elveszett,
mámorosan az elgyötört mocsokból
kikényszerített üdvösségüket!
De gyönyörük csak el se élvezett még,
hogy megfogamzott bennük a gyanú:
először csak a szájuk keserült el,
majd szívük lett iszonyú szomorú.

A tolongásból hirtelen kiálltak,
és úgy figyelték, szinte józanúl,
a nyomorukat eláruló mámor
mint járja őket keresztűl-kasúl.
És eleresztve magukat egészen,
csak arra vártak már, hogy szerveik
beteljesítsék, elvégezve rajtuk
a gyönyör végső tévedéseit.

Akárhová, csak szabadulni innét!
Csak menekülni, szökni mielébb!
Kiüldözött, hogy még felénk se villant,
hozzánk se ért az izzó csőcselék.
Köröskörűl a mozdulatlan bánya.
Csak haza már! Alant a folyamon
egy hajó úszhatott el a közelben,
hogy csupa füst lett és csupa korom

a fölfutó kijárat. Át a réten!
A dombokat mohón szökellve át
a lángoló betonra. Majd a villák!
A zölden visszaáradó világ.
A lóversenytér deszkakerítése,
s a deszkaközök sortüze után
a kertek alól kiájuló hőség,
s a hirtelenül ránkszakadt magány.

34

And, morsel for morsel, they took back
what along with them was lost for good:
the salvation they had somehow wrested,
rapturously, out of that harrowed filth!
Yet hardly had enjoyment run its course,
but that in them suspicion was conceived:
first only their mouths got a bitter taste,
then their hearts grew hideously sad.

Suddenly they stepped out of the tussle,
and so they watched, all but sober,
how the rapture betraying their misery
pervaded them through and through and all over.
And, letting go of themselves altogether,
now they only waited that their organs
should fulfill, executing upon them,
sensuous enjoyment's final errors.

No matter where: let's get away from here!
The sooner, the better: let's flee, be gone!
Not even glinting toward or touching us,
the white-hot rabble chased us out.
All around us the sand pit, motionless.
Let's just get home! Down, along the river,
a ship must have floated past nearby,
as the upward-sloping exit became covered

with smoke and soot. On across the meadow!
Greedily leaping over the hills,
onto the flaming concrete. Then the villas!
The world in its green, back-flooding heat.
After the plank-board fence of the race course
and the machine-gun fire of the chinks,
the heat, fainting from among the gardens,
and, collapsing on us, loneliness.

A lombok színe egyszerre kiégett,
és elborult a tüzük az uton.
Az arcunk és a kezünk is sötét lett,
és velünk együtt a paradicsom.
Hátunk megett a kocogató kannák,
s a szakadozó, poros fák között
már fölmerült az alkonyati város:
Frankfurt — 1945.

All at once, the color of the foliage
burned out; spreading on the road, its fires.
Our faces and hands, too, became dark,
and, together with us, paradise.
Behind our backs, among the knocking cans
and dust-covered trees that tear and grieve,
there now emerged the city in dusk:
Frankfurt—1945.

ARANYKORI TÖREDÉK

U. E.-nek

Öröm előzi, hirtelen öröm,
ama szemérmes, szép anarchia!
Nyitott a táj, zavartan is sima,
a szélsikálta torlaszos tetőkre,
a tenger kőre, háztetőre látni:
az alkonyati rengeteg ragyog.
Kimondhatatlan jól van, ami van.
Minden tetőről látni a napot.

Az össze-vissza zűrzavar kitárul,
a házakon s a házak tűzfalán,
a világvégi üres kutyaólban
aranykori és ugyanaz a nyár!
És ugyanaz a lüktető öröm;
dobog, dobog a forró semmiben,
ellök magától, eltaszít szivem
és esztelen szorít, szorít magához!

Mi készül itt e tenger ragyogásból?
Ha lehunyom is, süti a szemem;
mi kívül izzott, belül a pupillán,
itt izzít csak igazán, idebenn!
A világ is csak vele fényesűl,
az örömtől, aminek neve sincsen.
Mint vesztőhelyen, olyan vakitó
és olyan édes. Úgy igazi minden.

38

FRAGMENT FROM THE GOLDEN AGE

For E. U.

Joy precedes it, sudden joy,
that modest, beautiful anarchy!
The land is open, smooth even when disturbed;
you look out on the windscrubbed, barricaded roofs,
on the ocean of roofs and stone:
the twilight wilderness gleams.
What is, is unspeakably good.
From every roof you can see the sun.

Chaotic hubbub opens wide,
on the houses, the houses' firewalls;
in the empty kennel, at world's end,
summer is the same, of the age of gold!
And it's that same, same pulsing joy,
it throbs, it beats in the sizzling void;
my heart throws me, tosses me away,
and squeezes me to itself, out of its mind!

What emerges here, from this sea of radiance?
Even when I close them, it burns my eyes;
what outside is white-hot—inside the pupil
is where it's incandescent: here, inside!
It's only with it the world turns bright,
of joy, which is always shy of a name.
As at a gallows, so blinding it is,
and so sweet. It's how all things are made.

A SZERELEM SIVATAGA

Egy híd, egy forró betonút,
üríti zsebeit a nappal,
rendre kirakja mindenét.
Magad vagy a kataton alkonyatban.

Mint gyűrött gödör feneke a táj;
izzó hegek a káprázó homályban.
Alkonyodik. Dermeszt a ragyogás,
vakít a nap. Sosem felejtem, nyár van.

Nyár van és villámló meleg.
Állnak, s tudom, szárnyuk se rebben,
a szárnyasok, mint égő kerubok
a bedeszkázott, szálkás ketrecekben.

Emlékszel még? Először volt a szél;
aztán a föld; aztán a ketrec.
Tűz és ganaj. És néhanap
pár szárnycsapás, pár üres reflex.

És szomjúság. Én akkor inni kértem.
Hallom ma is a lázas kortyokat,
és tehetetlen tűröm, mint a kő,
és kioltom a káprázatokat.

Esztendők múlnak, évek, s a remény —
mint szalma közt kidöntött pléhedény.

LOVE'S DESERT

A bridge, a hot concrete road;
daytime empties its pockets,
displays, piece by piece, all it has.
You're alone in the catatonic twilight.

The land: like the bottom of a rumpled pit;
incandescent scars in the twilight glare.
Dusk falls. The brilliance numbs,
the sun blinds. I never forget it's summer.

It's summer and lightning heat.
They stand; I know: not even their wings
flail, the poultry—like burning cherubim
in the boarded-up, splinter-filled coops.

Remember still? First there was the wind,
then earth, then the chicken coop.
Fire and dung. And, once in a great while,
a few wing-beats—some empty reflexes.

And thirst. I then asked for a drink.
Today, I still hear the feverish gulps,
and helplessly I endure, like stone,
and extinguish any and all brilliance.

Years go by, years, and hope—
as in straw, an upset tin cup.

DÉL

Örökkétartó pillanat!
Vad szívverésem alig győzi csöndjét,
csak nagysokára, akkor is alig
rebben egyet a meglepett öröklét.
Majd újra vár, latolva mozdulatlan,
vadállati figyelme ezt meg azt,
majd az egészet egyből átkutatja,
nyugalmával hol itt, hol ott nyomaszt.
Egy házat próbál végre messze-messze,
méternyire a semmiség előtt
megvillogtatja. Eltökélten aztán,
hirtelen rá egy egész sor tetőt!
Közeledik, jön, jön a ragyogás
egy óriási közérzet egében —
Céltalanul fölvesz egy kavicsot,
és félrenéz a hajdani szemérem.
Mi látnivaló akad is azon,
hogy megérkezik valahol a nap,
és ellep, mint a vér, a melege,
hogy odatartott nyakszirtemre csap —
Emelkedik az elragadtatás!
Várakozom. Növekvő fényességben
köztem, s egy távol nádas rajza közt
mutál vékonyka földi jelenlétem.

NOON

Moment that lasts forever!
My wild heartbeat can hardly bear its silence:
only at long last, and even then, surprised
eternity scarcely flaps its wing.
Then it waits again, pondering motionless;
its wild-animal attentiveness
searches this, that, and the whole at once,
oppresses, with its calm, now here, now there.
Finally, far off, it tries a house:
at a meter's length, before Nothingness, it
makes it glint. Then, determined,
suddenly a whole row of roofs!
It comes, comes, brilliance approaches
in the sky of a gigantic overall feeling—
aimlessly, modesty of times past
picks up a pebble and looks to the side.
Just what is there to gape at
if the sun arrives somewhere
and, like blood, its warmth covers you,
if it slaps me on my held-out nape ... .
Rapture lifts!
I wait. In growing brightness,
between me and the outline of a distant marsh,
my gaunt earthly presence transforms.

JELENÉSEK VIII. 7.

és lát az isten égő mennyeket
s a menny szinén madarak szárnya-röptét
és látja mint merűlnek mind alább
a tűzkorongon átkerűlni gyöngék

és véges-végig mint a rézveres
olyan szinűt dirib-darabra törtet
hol nem találni mától egy kapást
a földet látja mégegyszer a földet

a pusztaságot és a zűrzavart
lovaskocsit keresve hol kigázol
de látja isten nincsen arra mód
kitörni út remény e látomásból!

REVELATION 8:7

and god does behold heavens aflame
and along the heavens birds' wing-and-flight
and he beholds how they sink ever lower
those too weak to pass the disc of fire

and end-to-end resembling copper-red
things so colored he smashes into bits
where from this day you cannot find a hoeman
once again it's earth he sees the fields

—looking for a horse cart breaking out—
the desolation overall confusion
but god sees that there just is no way
road hope for a breakout from this vision!

APOKRIF

1.

Mert elhagyatnak akkor mindenek.

Külön kerül az egeké, s örökre
a világvégi esett földeké,
s megint külön a kutyaólak csöndje.
A levegőben menekvő madárhad.
És látni fogjuk a kelő napot,
mint tébolyult pupilla néma és
mint figyelő vadállat, oly nyugodt.

De virrasztván a számkivettetésben,
mert nem alhatom akkor éjszaka,
hányódom én, mint ezer levelével,
és szólok én, mint éjidőn a fa:

Ismeritek az évek vonulását,
az évekét a gyűrött földeken?
És értitek a múlandóság ráncát,
ismeritek törődött kézfejem?
És tudjátok nevét az árvaságnak?
És tudjátok, miféle fájdalom
tapossa itt az örökös sötétet
hasadt patákon, hártyás lábakon?
Az éjszakát, a hideget, a gödröt,
a rézsut forduló fegyencfejet,
ismeritek a dermedt vályukat,
a mélyvilági kínt ismeritek?

APOCRYPHA

1.

Because then all, all shall be abandoned.

Separate comes the heavens' silence, and forever
the fields', fallen, of doomsday fall,
and separate again the silence of the kennels.
Up in the air, a fleeing host of birds.
And we shall see the rising sun,
it's mute as the insane pupil of an eye,
and as a watchful wild animal, so tranquil.

Yet, keeping vigil in the state of exile,
because I then cannot sleep at night,
I toss, as does with its thousand leaves
the tree at night and, like, it, I speak:

Do you know the passing of the years,
of the years, out on the wrinkled land?
And do you understand mortality's wrinkle,
do you know the careworn back of my hand?
And do you know the name of orphanhood?
And are you acquainted with the pain
that here treads and treads the eternal darkness
on cloven hooves and webbed feet?
The night, the cold, the ditch,
the sidelong-turning convict's head,
do you know the troughs, frozen stiff,
planet-deep torment, do you know it?

Feljött a nap. Vesszőnyi fák sötéten
a haragos ég infravörösében.

Így indulok. Szemközt a pusztulással
egy ember lépked hangtalan.
Nincs semmije, árnyéka van.
Meg botja van. Meg rabruhája van.

2.

Ezért tanultam járni! Ezekért
a kései, keserü léptekért.

S majd este lesz, és rámkövül sarával
az éjszaka, s én húnyt pillák alatt
őrzöm tovább e vonulást, e lázas
fácskákat s ágacskáikat.
Levelenként a forró, kicsi erdőt.
Valamikor a paradicsom állt itt.
Félálomban újuló fájdalom:
hallani óriási fáit!

Haza akartam, hazajutni végül,
ahogy megjött ő is a Bibliában.
Irtóztató árnyam az udvaron.
Törődött csönd, öreg szülők a házban.
S már jönnek is, már hívnak is, szegények
már sírnak is, ölelnek botladozva.
Visszafogad az ősi rend.
Kikönyöklök a szeles csillagokra —

The sun is up. Trees, like willow wands, dark
in the infrared of an angry sky.

So I start out. Face to face with doom
a man takes his steps, without a sound.
He has nothing; he has a shadow.
And a walking stick. And a prison uniform.

2.

For this I learned to walk! For these
belated, bitter steps.

And it will be evening, and night will petrify on me
with its mud and, under closed eyelashes,
I go on guarding this movement, these feverish
little trees and their small branches.
Leaf by leaf the torrid, tiny forest.
Paradise stood here once.
In half-dream, pain renewed—
you can hear its gigantic trees!

I wanted to reach home, home at last,
as he too arrived in the Bible.
My ghastly shadow in the courtyard.
Careworn silence, old parents in the house.
And now they come, and they call me, the poor dears
cry now, they embrace me, stumbling.
The old order receives me back.
I prop my elbows on the windswept stars ... .

Csak most az egyszer szólhatnék veled,
kit úgy szerettem. Év az évre,
de nem lankadtam mondani,
mit kisgyerek sír deszkarésbe,
a már-már elfuló reményt,
hogy megjövök és megtalállak.
Torkomban lüktet közeled.
Riadt vagyok, mint egy vadállat.

Szavaidat, az emberi beszédet
én nem beszélem. Élnek madarak,
kik szívszakadva menekülnek mostan
az ég alatt, a tüzes ég alatt.
Izzó mezőbe tűzdelt árva lécek,
és mozdulatlan égő ketrecek.
Nem értem én az emberi beszédet,
és nem beszélem a te nyelvedet.
Hazátlanabb az én szavam a szónál!
Nincs is szavam.
                      Iszonyu terhe
omlik alá a levegőn,
hangokat ad egy torony teste.

Sehol se vagy. Mily üres a világ.
Egy kerti szék, egy kinnfeledt nyugágy.
Éles kövek közt árnyékom csörömpöl.
Fáradt vagyok. Kimeredek a földből.

Could I but have words with you just this once,
whom I loved so much. Year upon year,
but I did not grow faint of saying
what a small child weeps into the chinks:
hope, on the point of drowning,
that I'll reach home and find you.
Your nearness pulses in my throat.
Like a wild beast, I am scared, alert.

I am not one to speak your words—
human language. There live birds
who, heartbroken, now take their flight
under the skies, the fiery skies.
Lone laths, planted in incandescent fields,
and cages burning, motionless.
I don't understand human speech,
and of your language I speak not a word.
My word is more homeless than the Word!
I *have* no word.
                    Its dreadful weight
tumbles down through air,
a tower's body gives off sounds.

You are nowhere. How empty the world.
A garden chair, a deck chair left outside.
Among sharp-edged stones my shadow clatters.
I am tired. I tower out of the ground.

3.

Látja Isten, hogy állok a napon.
Látja árnyam kövön és keritésen.
Lélekzet nélkül látja állani
árnyékomat a levegőtlen présben.

Akkorra én már mint a kő vagyok;
halott redő, ezer rovátka rajza,
egy jó tenyérnyi törmelék
akkorra már a teremtmények arca.

És könny helyett az arcokon a ráncok,
csorog alá, csorog az üres árok.

3.

God sees that I am standing in the sun.
He sees my shadow on stone and on fence.
He sees my shadow standing breathless
in the airless press.

By then I am just like stone;
dead grooves, outlines of a thousand creases,
a good palmful of rubble—this,
by then, is what is left of creatures' faces.

And instead of tears on faces, wrinkles;
it runs, the empty ditch—on down it trickles.

NÉGYSOROS

Alvó szegek a jéghideg homokban.
Plakátmagányban ázó éjjelek.
Égve hagytad a folyosón a villanyt.
Ma ontják véremet.

FOUR-LINER

Sleeping nails in the ice-cold sand.
Nights soaking in poster-solitude.
You left the light on in the hallway.
Today they are shedding my blood.

EGY ARCKÉP ALÁ

Kihűl a nap az alkonyi grafitban.
Tágasságával, mélységeivel
a néma tenger arcomba világít.
Öreg vagyok. Nem hiszek semmiben.

Öreg vagyok, lerombolt arcomon
csupán a víz ijesztő pusztasága.
A szürkület gránitpora. Csupán
a pórusok brutális csipkefátyla!

Hullámverés. Aztán a puha éj
boldogtalan zajai. Vak rovar,
magam vagyok a rámsötétedő,
a világárva papundekliban.

És egyedül a feneketlen ágyban.
És egyedül a párnáim között.
Magam vagyok az örökös magányban.
Akár a víz. Akár az anyaföld.

UNDER A PORTRAIT

The sun cools in the graphite of dusk.
With its spaciousness, its depths,
the mute sea shines into my face.
I am old. I believe in nothing.

I am old; on my demolished face,
purely water's frightening desolation.
Twilight's granite dust. Only
the pores' brutal veil of lace!

Beating of waves. Then soft night's
unhappy noises. A blind worm,
I am alone in the darkening,
world-orphaned cardboard.

And alone in the bottomless bed.
And among my pillows, alone.
I am alone in the eternal solitude.
Just like water. Like mother loam.

FÉLMÚLT

Ted Hughesnak

Megérkezik és megmered,
kiűl a hamunéma falra:
egyetlen óriás ütés
a hold. Halálos csönd a magja.

Összetöri az utakat,
összetöri a hold sütése.
És ketté tépi a falat.
Fehér zuhog a feketére.

Villámlik és villámlik és
villámlik a fekete nappal.
Fehér zuhog és fekete.
Fésülködöl a mágneses viharban.

Fésülködöl a fényes csendben,
a félmultnál is éberebb tükörben.

Fésülködöl tükrödben szótlan,
akár egy üvegkoporsóban.

IMPERFECT TENSE

For Ted Hughes

It arrives, grows rigid,
sits on the cinder-mute wall:
a single, enormous blow—
the moon. Deathly silence its core.

It shatters the roads,
it shatters them—the moon's light.
And tears the wall in half.
White pours down on black.

Black daylight lightens,
lightens and lightens.
White pours down, and black.
You are combing your hair in the magnetic storm.

You are combing your hair in the gleaming silence,
in a mirror even more alert than the imperfect tense.

You are combing your hair in your mirror, speechless,
as in a glass coffin.

NOVEMBERI ELÍZIUM

A lábadozás ideje. Megtorpansz
a kert előtt. Nyugalmas sárga fal
kolostorcsendje háttered. Kezes
szellőcske indul a füvek közűl,
s mintha szentelt olajjal kenegetnék,
érzékeid öt meggyötört sebe
enyhületet érez és gyógyulást.

Bátortalan vagy s ujjongó! Igen,
gyermekien áttetsző tagjaiddal
a nagyranőtt kendőben és kabátban,
mint Karamazov Aljosa, olyan vagy.

És olyan is, mint ama szelidek,
kik mint a gyermek, igen, olyan is vagy,
oly boldog is, hisz semmit sem akarsz már,
csak ragyogni a novemberi napban,
és illatozni toboz-könnyüen.
Csak melegedni, mint az üdvözültek.

Szigliget, 1958. november

ELYSIUM IN NOVEMBER

The time for convalescence. You stop in your tracks
in front of the garden. Your backdrop is a quiet
yellow wall's monastery-silence. Gentle
small breeze starts from the grasses,
and, as though anointed with holy oil,
your senses' five tortured wounds
feel relief and healing.

You are shy and jubilant! Yes,
with your limbs, translucent as a child's,
in the overgrown scarf and topcoat,
you are just like Alyosha Karamazov.

And you are also like those tame ones,
those who resemble children, yes, like them too,
and just as happy, since you want nothing any more,
only to gleam in the November sun,
and to be fragrant, light as a pine cone.
Only to warm yourself, like the blessed.

Szigliget, November 1958

from *Metropolitan Icons* (1970)

UTÓSZÓ

Pierre Emmanuelnek

Emlékszel még? Az arcokon.
Emlékszel még? Az üres árok.
Emlékszel még? Csorog alá.
Emlékszel még? A napon állok.

A Paris Journalt olvasod.
Tél van azóta, téli éjjel.
Megteritesz a közelemben,
megágyazol a holdsütésben.

Lélekzet nélkül vetkezel
éjszakáján a puszta háznak.
Inged, ruhád leengeded.
Mezítelen sírkő a hátad.

Boldogtalan erejü kép.
Van itt valaki?
                Éber álom:
felelet nélkül átkelek
a tükrök mélyén heverő szobákon.

Ez hát az arcom, ez az arc?
A fény, a csönd, az ítélet csörömpöl
ahogy az arcom, ez a kő
röpűl felém a hófehér tükörből!

S a lovasok! A lovasok!
Bánt a homály és sért a lámpa.
Vékony sugárka víz csorog
a mozdulatlan porcelánra.

AFTERWORD

For Pierre Emmanuel

Do you still remember? On the faces.
Do you still remember? The empty ditch.
Do you still remember? It's trickling down.
Do you still remember? I'm standing in the sun.

You're reading the *Paris-Journal*.
Since then it's been winter, winter night.
You're setting the table near me,
making the bed in the moonlight.

Without breath you're undressing
in the night of the deserted house.
You let down your shirt, your clothes.
Your back is a bare tombstone.

A portrait of unhappy power.
Is someone there?
                    Sleepless dream:
there's no answer—I cross rooms
that lounge in the mirrors' depths.

Is this, then, my face, this face?
Light, silence, judgment shatter
as my face, this stone
flies at me from the snowwhite mirror!

And the horsemen! The horsemen!
Dusk hurts, the lamp injures me.
A thin ray of water dribbles
on the motionless porcelain.

Csukott ajtókon zörgetek.
Sötét szobád, akár az akna.
A falakon hideg lobog.
Sírásom mázolom a falra.

Segítsetek hófödte háztetők!
Éjszaka van. Ragyogjon, ami árva,
a semmi napja mielőtt
megjelenne. Ragyogjatok hiába!

Falnak támasztom fejemet.
Mindenfelől az irgalomnak
marék havát nyujtja felém
egy halott város a halottnak.

Szerettelek! Egy kiáltás, egy sóhaj,
egy menekülő felhő elfutóban.
S a lovasok zuhogó, sűrü trappban
megjönnek a csatakos virradatban.

I rattle on closed doors.
Your dark room—just like a mine shaft.
On the walls cold flutters.
I smear my weeping on the wall.

Help me, snow-covered roofs!
It's night. Let what is orphaned gleam
before the day of nothingness
should appear. Gleam—in vain!

I lean my head against the wall.
From everywhere it reaches to me
mercy's handful of snow—
to the dead, a dead city.

I loved you! A shout, a sigh,
a fugitive cloud on the run.
And the horsemen, in falling, thick hoofpatter,
arrive in the rainbeaten dawn.

INTROITUSZ

Ki nyitja meg a betett könyvet?
Ki szegi meg a töretlen időt?
Lapozza fel hajnaltól-hajnalig
emelve és ledöntve lapjait?

Az ismeretlen tűzvészébe nyúlni
ki merészel közülünk? S ki merészel
a csukott könyv leveles sürüjében,
ki mer kutatni? S hogy mer puszta kézzel?

És ki nem fél közülünk? Ki ne félne,
midőn szemét az Isten is lehúnyja,
és leborúlnak minden angyalok,
és elsötétűl minden kreatúra?

A bárány az, ki nem fél közülünk,
egyedül ő, a bárány, kit megöltek.
Végigkocog az üvegtengeren
és trónra száll. És megnyitja a könyvet.

INTROIT

Who will open the closed book?
Who shall breach unbroken time?
Open it, lifting, letting fall
its leaves from dawn until dawn?

Who among us dare reach into the
wildfire of the unknown? And who dare
search among the leafy thicket
of the closed book? And with his bare hand?

And who among us is not afraid? Who would not be
when God himself closes his eyes,
and all the angels fall prostrate,
and all creation grows dark?

The Lamb is the one among us, unafraid,
he alone, the Lamb, whom they killed.
He jogs across the ocean of glass
and mounts the throne. And opens the book.

KZ-ORATÓRIUM

Szín: üres színpad vagy koncertdobogó. A kórus félkör alakban a színpad két oldalán foglal helyet, középütt keskeny utat hagyva. Fölül vízszintesen kifeszített hangversenylámpák.

Szereplők: KISFIÚ; ÖREGASSZONY; R. M., fiatal lány. Mindhárman KZ-lakók.

A zenekar hangolása közben először R. M. jelenik meg, majd a KISFIÚ, utoljára az ÖREGASSZONY. R. M. csíkos rabruhát visel, haja rövidre nyírva; az Öregasszony feketében van; a Kisfiún szürke porköpeny. Égő gyertyával kezükben mindhárman a színpad elejére, középre állnak. Előttük kottaállványon a szövegkönyv, melyet előadás közben szabad kezükkel ők maguk lapoznak. A kisfiú áll középen, jobbra tőle a lány, balra az öregasszony. A zenekar elcsendesedik. Szünet.

R. M.
Én Varsóból való vagyok.

ÖREGASSZONY
Én Prágából.

KISFIÚ
Én nem tudom, honnan.

ÖREGASSZONY
(*Fejét fölütve.*)
Mintha szegeket ráztak volna.

R. M.
Mintha szegeket ráztam volna!

70

KZ ORATORIO

Scene: empty stage or concert platform. The Chorus takes its place in a semicircle on both sides of the stage, leaving a narrow path in the middle. Horizontally mounted stage lights overhead.

Characters: YOUNG BOY; OLD WOMAN; M. R., a young girl. All three are KZ inmates.

While the orchestra tunes, first M. R. appears, then the YOUNG BOY, the OLD WOMAN last. M. R. is wearing a striped prison uniform, with her hair trimmed short; the OLD WOMAN is dressed in black; the YOUNG BOY has on a gray smock. With lighted candles in their hands, all three come and stand in front of the stage, in the middle. Before each, on a music stand, the script, whose pages they themselves turn with their free hands during the performance. The young boy stands in the middle, to his right the girl, to his left the old woman. The orchestra grows silent. Pause.

M. R.
I'm from Warsaw.

OLD WOMAN
I'm from Prague.

YOUNG BOY
I don't know where I'm from.

OLD WOMAN
(*Her head perked.*)
It's as if they had shaken nails.

M. R.
It's as if I had shaken nails!

71

KISFIÚ
Akkor láttam először éjszakát!

ÖREGASSZONY
Nem ébredtek fel a szegek.

R. M.
Én ordítoztam a dobozban!

ÖREGASSZONY
Nem ébredtem fel soha többé.

R. M.
Én Varsóból való vagyok.

ÖREGASSZONY
Én Prágából.

KISFIÚ
Én nem tudom, honnan.

ÖREGASSZONY
Éjszaka volt, amikor elhagytuk a várost.

R. M.
Kivilágítva, elfeledve.

ÖREGASSZONY
Kopogtak a jégüres csillagok.

R. M.
Kopogtak a jégüres villanykörték.

ÖREGASSZONY
Mintha szegeket ráztak volna.

YOUNG BOY
That's when I first saw night!

OLD WOMAN
The nails didn't wake up.

M. R.
I hollered in the box!

OLD WOMAN
I never woke up any more.

M. R.
I'm from Warsaw.

OLD WOMAN
I'm from Prague.

YOUNG BOY
I don't know where I'm from.

OLD WOMAN
It was night when we left the city.

M. R.
Lit up, forgotten.

OLD WOMAN
The ice-empty stars were tapping.

M. R.
The ice-empty light bulbs were tapping.

OLD WOMAN
It's as if they had shaken nails.

R. M.
Arcok, kezek. Kimerült törmelék.
Zuhogott a nyíltszini massza.

ÖREGASSZONY
Fények egy elfelejtett arcon.

R. M.
Ráncok egy soselátott arcban.

ÖREGASSZONY
Prága, csak ennyi voltál?

R. M.
Kivilágítva, elfeledve.

KISFIÚ
Ezentúl ne szóljatok hozzám.

R. M.
Életemben nem láttam házat!
Fenyők közt állt egy fasor végén.
Ragyogtak az ablakai.
Nem érintettem a kezemmel.
Nagyon vigyázva megérintem.

Felejts el, felejts el, szerelmem!
Kit érdekel a fatörzsnek dőlt állat?

ÖREGASSZONY
A holdsütésben írnokok.

R. M.
Templomok és temetőkertek.

M. R.
Faces, hands. Exhausted rubble.
In torrents the mid-scene mass rained down.

OLD WOMAN
Lights on a forgotten face.

M. R.
Wrinkles in a face never seen.

OLD WOMAN
Prague: is this all you were?

M. R.
Lit up, forgotten.

YOUNG BOY
From now on, don't speak to me.

M. R.
In all my life, I never saw a house!
It stood among firs, at the end of a tree-lined lane.
Its windows glistened.
I didn't touch it with my hand.
Very cautiously, I'm touching it.

Forget me, forget me, love!
Who cares about a beast leaning against a treetrunk?

OLD WOMAN
In the moonlight, scribes.

M. R.
Churches and graveyards.

ÖREGASSZONY
Diófák, porkolábparasztok.

R. M.
Félálomakták; tű és cérna.

ÖREGASSZONY
Halálos csend.

R. M.
Gótbetűk.

ÖREGASSZONY
Németország.

KISFIÚ
Nagyon messze és egészen közel
a kőasztalon feküdt valaki.

ÖREGASSZONY
Olyan volt, mintha virágház lett volna,
de nem voltak benne virágok.
Egyetlen hosszú folyosó;
vályogfalak, de a föld melegével.
A folyosó kiszélesült a végén,
s világított, mint egy monstrancia.

R. M.
(*Mint egy másik történetben, fokozott egyszerűséggel.*)
Hol volt, hol nem volt,
élt egyszer egy magányos farkas.
Magányosabb az angyaloknál.

Elvetődött egyszer egy faluba,
és beleszeretett az első házba, amit meglátott.

76

OLD WOMAN
Walnut trees, turnkey peasants.

M. R.
Light-sleep paperwork; needle and thread.

OLD WOMAN
Deathly silence.

M. R.
Gothic lettering.

OLD WOMAN
Germany.

YOUNG BOY
Very far and quite near,
someone lay on the stone table.

OLD WOMAN
It was just like a greenhouse,
only there were no flowers in it.
A single long corridor;
adobe walls, but with earth's warmth.
At its end the corridor widened,
and gave off light, like a monstrance.

M. R.
(*As if in another story, with heightened simplicity.*)
Once upon a time
there lived a lone wolf.
Lonelier than the angels.

He once chanced to come to a village,
and fell in love with the first house he saw.

Már a falát is megszerette,
a kőmüvesek simogatását,
de az ablak megállította.

A szobában emberek ültek.
Istenen kívül soha senki
olyan szépnek nem látta őket,
mint ez a tisztaszivü állat.

Éjszaka aztán be is ment a házba,
megállt a szoba közepén,
s nem mozdult onnan soha többé.

Nyitott szemmel állt egész éjszaka,
s reggel is, mikor agyonverték.

KISFIÚ
Ugye, mi halottak vagyunk?

R. M.
Olyan volt, mintha virágház lett volna,
de nem voltak benne virágok.
Egyetlen sötét folyosó;
vályogfalak, de a föld melegével.
Délután volt, úgy három óra.
A folyosó kiszélesült a végén
s világitott, mint egy monstrancia —

A teteje üvegből lehetett,
mert megrekedt benne a napsugár.
Mezítlenűl és végérvényesen
a kőasztalon feküdt valaki.

ÖREGASSZONY
A holdsütésben írnokok.

He came to like its very walls,
the caresses of the stonemasons,
but the window made him stop.

People sat in the room.
Besides God, no one had ever
seen them so beautiful
as this pure-hearted animal.

At night, then, he entered the house,
stopped in the middle of the room,
and never stirred from there any more.

All night he stood, his eyes open,
and in the morning, too, when they beat him to death.

YOUNG BOY
We're dead, aren't we?

M. R.
It was just like a greenhouse,
only there were no flowers in it.
A single dark corridor;
adobe walls, but with earth's warmth.
It was afternoon, say, three o'clock.
As its end the corridor widened,
and gave off light, like a monstrance ... .

Its roof must have been of glass,
for sunlight got trapped in it.
Naked and with finality,
someone lay on the stone table.

OLD WOMAN
In the moonlight, scribes.

R. M.
Templomok és temetőkertek.

ÖREGASSZONY
Diófák; porkolábparasztok.

R. M.
Félálomakták, tű és cérna.

ÖREGASSZONY
Egyetlen óriás ütés!

R. M.
Halottak magnéziumlángban.

ÖREGASSZONY
Halálos csend.

R. M.
Gótbetűk.

ÖREGASSZONY
Németország.

R. M.
Későre jár. Márcsak a rabruha
kifoszló cérnaszála van velem.
Letépem és számba veszem a cérnát.
Itt fekszem holtan a nyelvem hegyén.

ÖREGASSZONY
Drágáim, ne ítéljetek!

M. R.
Churches and graveyards.

OLD WOMAN
Walnut trees; turnkey peasants.

M. R.
Light-sleep paperwork, needle and thread.

OLD WOMAN
A single, enormous blow!

M. R.
Corpses in magnesium light.

OLD WOMAN
Deathly silence.

M. R.
Gothic lettering.

OLD WOMAN
Germany.

M. R.
It's getting late. Now only the prison garment's
frayed thread is with me.
I tear off the thread and put it in my mouth.
Here I lie, dead, on the tip of my tongue.

OLD WOMAN
Dear ones, don't judge me!

KISFIÚ
Hét kocka van.
Az elsőt nem tudom.
A második: utak és messzeség.
A harmadikban katonák.
A negyedik kockában mi vagyunk.
Az ötödikben: éhség és kenyér!
A hatodik kockában csönd van.
A hetedik kockát nem ismerem.

R. M.
Azt álmodom, fölébredek.

ÖREGASSZONY
Próbáld meg, drágám, mit veszíthetsz? Hátha!

R. M.
Nagyon félek, hogy elveszíthetem. (*Szünet.*)
Átsietek a kihalt udvaron.

ÖREGASSZONY
Elvesztél! Nincs mit elveszítened!

R. M.
Úgy érzem, itt van, egész közel.

ÖREGASSZONY
Közel, ahogy csak mi tudunk szeretni.

R. M.
Itt van. Eláll a szívverésem.

ÖREGASSZONY
Törd rá az ajtót! Nekünk már szabad.

YOUNG BOY
There are seven cubes.
Of the first, I know nothing.
The second: roads and distance.
In the third, soldiers.
In the fourth cube: we ourselves.
In the fifth: hunger and bread!
In the sixth cube, there's silence.
The seventh cube I don't know.

M. R.
I dream that I'm waking up.

OLD WOMAN
Try it, dear; what can you lose? Maybe!

M. R.
I'm terribly afraid I may lose him. (*Pause.*)
I'm hurrying across the deserted courtyard.

OLD WOMAN
You're lost! You have nothing to lose!

M. R.
I feel he's here, very close by.

OLD WOMAN
Close, as only we can love.

M. R.
He's here. My heartbeat stops.

OLD WOMAN
Break down his door! We may do it now.

R. M.

Sírok. Itt van az arcomon.

Itt van minden, mi enyém s nem enyém.

ÖREGASSZONY

Igen, csak azt az egyet tudhatnánk, hogy

végül is megtörhetjük-e,

nem a magunkét, a másik magányát;

az áldozatét, aki fél,

a gyilkosét, ki nem érzi, hogy ölt!

azét, ki már nem is mer tudni rólunk.

R. M.

Itt patakzik minden az arcomon.

KISFIÚ

Az első kockát nem tudom.

A második: utak és messzeség!

Sötét utak és üres messzeség.

ÖREGASSZONY

(*Kezét a levegőnek támasztva.*) Havazni kezd.

Prágában tél van.

Üvegtető alatt kis asztal áll.

Billeg az egyik lába.

Forog belűl az óraszerkezet.

Valamikor azt hittem, itt vagyok.

KISFIÚ

A negyedik kockában mi vagyunk.

R. M.

Kivilágítva, elfelejtve.

M. R.
I'm crying. Here he is, on my face.
Here is all that is mine, and not mine.

OLD WOMAN
Yes; if we could but know that one thing:
whether in the end we may break in,
not on our own, on the loneliness of the other;
of the victim, the one who is afraid,
of the murderer, who doesn't feel he has killed!
of the one who dare not even know of us any more.

M. R.
Here streams everything, down my face.

YOUNG BOY
Of the first cube, I know nothing.
The second: roads and distance!
Dark roads and empty distance.

OLD WOMAN
(*Leaning her hand against the air.*) It's starting to snow.
In Prague it's winter.
Under a glass roof stands a small table.
One of its legs wobbles.
The clockwork twirls inside.
There was a time I believed I'm here.

YOUNG BOY
In the fourth cube: we ourselves.

M. R.
Lit up, forgotten.

ÖREGASSZONY
Átsietek a Szent Vencel téren. (*Szünet.*)
(*Mintegy magában beszélve.*) Emberek,
irgalmazzatok!

R. M.
Végkép magam.
  Márcsak a rabruhából
kifoszló cérnaszál maradt velem,
felöltve egy vonal iratlan sorsát.

Nincs semmi, csak a hely meg az idő,
hol utoljára számontartanak.

Csak én vagyok és ők. (*Szünet.*) Kik még alusznak.

ÖREGASSZONY
Drágáim, ne ítéljetek!
Úgy éltünk itten, mint a barmok.
Akár a disznók, térdeltünk a porban,
mégis mire nyelvünkre ért az étel,
szelíd volt az, akár az Isten teste.

KISFIÚ
A hatodik kockában csend van.

R. M.
Azt álmodom, felébredek.
Hihetetlenűl mély az éjszaka.
Alig vagyok.

    Egyetlen egy szoba,
egy ablak világít csak: az övé.
S az is üres.
    Mint összetört tükör

OLD WOMAN
I'm hurrying across St. Wenceslas Square. (*Pause.*)
(*As if talking to herself.*) People,
have mercy!

M. R.
With finality, by myself.
                    Now only the thread
fraying from the prison garment has stayed with me,
stitching up a line's unwritten fate.

There's nothing but the place and the time
where for one last time we're kept track of.

It's only me and them. (*Pause.*) Those still asleep.

OLD WOMAN
Dear ones, don't judge me!
We lived here just like cattle.
Just like hogs, we knelt in the dust,
and yet, by the time the food reached our tongues,
tame it was, like the body of God.

YOUNG BOY
In the sixth cube, there's silence.

M. R.
I dream that I'm waking up.
Night is incredibly deep.
I scarcely exist.

                    A single solitary room;
only one window is lit: his.
And that, too, is empty.
                    Like a shattered mirror,

hull a szobája, s nem bír földet érni!

Levelenként kell félrehajtanom
a puha erdőt. Mind megannyi seb.
Elalélok, hogy szép fejét kifejtem
az agyonázott levelek közűl.

Szebb, mint a legszebb fiatal lány –
Nincs többé erdő.   Mit akarsz még tőlünk?

A halálunkat, azt nem, azt nem adjuk.
Azt magunkhoz szorítjuk és nem adjuk.

KISFIÚ
A hetedik kockát nem ismerem.
*(Lassan induló omlás zaja, mintha üregek szakadtak volna le, s az üregekben
kövek záporoznának. Aztán az egész omlás egyszerre véget ér. A kórusból
jobbról is, balról is előlépnek ketten-hárman, tüzet vesznek, s elfújják az
Öregasszony, a Kisfiú s a Fiatal lány gyertyáját. Majd helyükre visszaállva
továbbadják a lángot az egész kórusnak.)*

R. M.
Milyen puha a levegő.
Csorgó eresz, barakfal, messzeség.
Boldogságig lelassult pusztulás.

KISFIÚ
A hatodik kockában csönd van.

R. M.
Valószinűtlenűl
gyenge pulzusok igyekeznek;
próbálnak megmaradni.

his room tumbles, and it cannot reach the ground!

Leaf by leaf I must bend aside
the soft forest. Each just like a wound.
I'm dozing off as I separate out his comely head
from among the deathly soaked leaves.

He's more beautiful than the comeliest of young girls ... .
There's no more forest.
What do you still want of us?

Our deaths—oh no, that we won't give.
We'll press it to ourselves, and we won't give it up.

YOUNG BOY
The seventh cube I don't know.
(*Noise of slowly starting landslide, as if abysses were caving in, and stones were showering in the depths. Then the whole landslide suddenly comes to an end. From the Chorus, from the left as from the right, two or three members step out front, take up fire, and blow out the candles of the Old Woman, the Young Boy, and the Girl. Then returning to their places, they hand the flame on to the rest of the Chorus.*)

M. R.
How soft the air is.
Trickling eaves, barrack walls, distance.
Devastation slowed to the point of blessedness.

YOUNG BOY
In the sixth cube, silence.

M. R.
Improbably
weak pulse-beats are making an effort;
they're trying to survive.

89

KISFIÚ
A hatodik kockában némaság van.

R. M.
Minden megáll. Varsóban este van.
Fehér pokróc borította az ágyam!

ÖREGASSZONY
Édeseim! Édeseim!

R. M.
Én sötét mennyországom.
(*A függőlámpák is kialszanak.*)

ÖREGASSZONY
Olyan volt, mint egy átlyuggatott tenyér.
Ragyogtak az ablakai.
Világitott a fasor végén.
A szobában emberek ültek.
Vonultunk az országuton.
A házat elfedik a fák.

R. M.
Késő re jár. Márcsak a rabruha
kifoszló cérnaszála van velem.
Letépem és számba veszem a cérnát.
Itt patakzik minden az arcomon.

KISFIÚ
A hetedik kockát nem ismerem.

R. M.
Csak én vagyok és ők, kik még alusznak.

YOUNG BOY
In the sixth cube, there's muteness.

M. R.
Everything comes to a halt. In Warsaw it's evening.
A white blanket covered my bed!

OLD WOMAN
Dear ones! Dear ones!

M. R.
My dark heaven.
(*The overhead lights go out as well.*)

OLD WOMAN
It was like a riddled palm.
Its windows gleamed.
It gave off light at the end of the tree-lined lane.
People sat in the room.
We pulled along the road.
Trees hide the house.

M. R.
It's getting late. Only the prison garment's
fraying thread is with me now.
I tear off the thread and put it in my mouth.
Here streams everything, down my face.

YOUNG BOY
The seventh cube I don't know.

M. R.
It's only me and them, those still asleep.

ÖREGASSZONY
A holdsütésben írnokok.

R. M.
Templomok és temetőkertek.

ÖREGASSZONY
Diófák; porkolábparasztok.

R. M.
Félálomakták, tű és cérna.

ÖREGASSZONY
Egyetlen óriás ütés!

R. M.
Halottak magnéziumfényben.

ÖREGASSZONY
Fények egy elfelejtett arcon.

R. M.
Ráncok egy soselátott arcban.

ÖREGASSZONY
Mintha szegeket ráztak volna.

R. M.
Mintha szegeket ráztam volna.

KISFIÚ
Először látok éjszakát!

R. M.
Én ordítoztam a dobozban!

OLD WOMAN
In the moonlight, scribes.

M. R.
Churches and graveyards.

OLD WOMAN
Walnut trees; turnkey peasants.

M. R.
Light-sleep paperwork, needle and thread.

OLD WOMAN
A single, enormous blow!

M. R.
Corpses in magnesium light.

OLD WOMAN
Lights on a forgotten face.

M. R.
Wrinkles in a face never seen.

OLD WOMAN
It's as if they had shaken nails.

M. R.
It's as if I had shaken nails.

YOUNG BOY
For the first time I'm seeing night!

M. R.
I hollered in the box!

ÖREGASSZONY
Nem ébredek fel soha többé.

KISFIÚ
(*Egy-két lépést előrelép. Kissé elkülönülve, s két kezét fürkészőn
maga elé emelve.*)
Boldogtalan a pillanat, mikor
fölfedezi az árva önmagát,
s arra gondol, hogy másnak is
fontos lehet e kéz, e görbeség,
s azontúl arra vágyik, hogy szeressék.

R. M.
Én Varsóból való vagyok.

ÖREGASSZONY
Én Prágából.

KISFIÚ
Én nem tudom, honnan.

(*A függőlámpák kigyulladnak.*)

OLD WOMAN
I'll never wake up any more.

YOUNG BOY
(*Takes a step or two forward. Off to the side a bit, and raising his two probing hands in front of him.*)
Unhappy the moment when
the orphan discovers himself,
and takes thought that this hand, this curve
could also be important for another,
and from then on he longs to be loved.

M. R.
I'm from Warsaw.

OLD WOMAN
I'm from Prague.

YOUNG BOY
I don't know where I'm from.

(*The overhead lights go on.*)

NAGYVÁROSI IKONOK

Déli 12 óra
Lakhatatlan, kiáltják, lakhatatlan!

Hajnali három
Megindulunk egy kőrakás felé,
és fölröpül mögüle egy madár.

Múzeum
A gyémántüres múzeum
közepében egy melltű lángol.
Lerombol és megörökít.
Hová jutunk e lángolásból?

A mozdulatlan karzatok?
Magányos kézelőd talán?
Lerombol és megörökít
a júniusi délután.

Szeptemberi sugárutak!
Szerelmem, szerelmem, szerelmem!
Megállnak a sugárutak.
Egyetemes sebek a kertben.

Te megpróbáltad azt, amit
senki se merészelt, te árva!
fényeskedjék neked az éj
öröküres monstranciája.

METROPOLITAN ICONS

Twelve Noon
Unlivable, they shout, unlivable!

Three A.M.
We start out toward a pile of stones,
and from behind it a bird flies up.

Museum
The diamond-empty museum —
in its midst, a brooch in flames.
It demolishes, perpetuates.
Where to, out of this flaming state?

The unmoving galleries?
Your cuff perhaps, the one alone?
It demolishes, perpetuates —
the June afternoon.

Boulevards in September!
My love, my love, my love!
The boulevards come to a halt.
Universal wounds in the garden.

You tried to undertake
what no one has dared, you orphan!
let it light for you, night's
eternally empty monstrance.

Kórus

A Kreatúra könyörög,
leroskad, megadja magát.
A Kreatúra, Az-Ami
könyörög, mutatja magát.

Chorus
Created Being implores,
collapses, surrenders.
All that is created—That Which
Implores—displays itself.

VAN GOGH

1.

Ők levetkőztek a sötétben,
ölelkeztek és elaludtak,
miközben te a ragyogásban
sírtál és mérlegeltél.

2.

Alkonyodott.
A rozoga melegben
papírközelbe ért a nap.
Minden megállt.
Állt ott egy vasgolyó is.

3.

"Világ báránya, lupus in fabula,
a jelenidő vitrinében égek!"

VAN GOGH

1.

They undressed in the dark,
embraced and fell asleep
while you, in the brilliance,
wept and considered.

2.

Dusk was falling.
In the precarious heat
the sun came paper-close.
Everything stopped.
An iron ball stood there as well.

3.

"Lamb of the world, lupus in fabula,
I am burning in the vitrine of the present tense!"

KIS ÉJIZENE

Virágcsokor
Óh, vesztőhelyek illata!

Párbeszéd
Eresszetek be, itt vagyok,
nyissatok ajtót, megérkeztem.

Nincs ajtó, mit megnyithatunk.
Nincs retesz, ami kirekesszen.

Éjfél
Elgurulnak az ismeretlen csöndben,
mélyen a csillagok alatt
elgurulnak
s megállanak
a mozdulatlan billiárdgolyók.

Mozart
Egy ház, egy udvar. Álmom és halálom.
Délszaki csönd, emlékezet.
Reflektorfény a falakon,
üresség és márványerek.

"Dans cette maison habita Mozart"
Mozart lakott itt valaha.
Egy vázában virágcsokor.

Óh, vesztőhelyek illata!

Párizs, 1963

A LITTLE NIGHT MUSIC

Bouquet of Flowers
O gallows-fragrance!

Dialogue
Let me in; I'm here;
open the door; I've arrived.

There's no door we could open.
No bolt to shut you out.

Midnight
They roll away in the unknown silence,
deep under the stars
they roll away
and stop,
the motionless billiard balls.

Mozart
A house, a courtyard. My dream and my death.
Southern silence, memory.
Searchlight-gleam on the walls,
emptiness and marble veins.

"Dans cette maison habita Mozart" —
Mozart lived here once.
In a vase a bouquet of flowers.

O gallows-fragrance!

Paris, 1963

FEHÉR PIÉTA

A fényérzékeny levegőben
csukott szemhéjak. Anya és fia.
Fehér kezek és még fehérebb ráncok.
Piéta és laterna mágika.

WHITE PIETÀ

In the light-sensitive air,
closed eyelids. Mother and son.
White hands and even whiter wrinkles.
Pietà and laterna magica.

PASSIÓ

Csak a vágóhíd melege,
muskátliszaga, puha máza,
csak a nap van. Üvegmögötti csöndben
lemosdanak a mészároslegények,
de ami történt, valahogy mégse tud végetérni.

PASSION

There are only the warmth of the slaughterhouse,
its geranium-smell, paint job soft to the touch;
there is only the sun. In silence behind glass
the butcher's assistants wash up,
but even so, somehow, what took place just cannot
come to an end.

A HÓHÉR NAPLÓJÁBÓL

Thomas Transtrőmernek

Egyszer történt, hogy meginogtam,
s elvesztve egyensúlyomat
a feneketlen és királyi csöndben
meg is történt, hogy meginogtam.

Különben csak az órák kettyegnek
egyre pontosabban,
egyre hangosabban.

Nem tudok meghalni többé,
mióta a gyémántokat visszahelyeztem a koronába.

FROM THE HENCHMAN'S DIARY

For Thomas Tranströmer

Once it happened that I staggered
and, losing my balance
in the bottomless and royal silence,
it did happen that I staggered.

Otherwise, only the clocks tick
ever more punctually,
ever louder.

I cannot die anymore,
ever since I replaced the diamonds in the crown.

SZENT LATOR

Törőcsik Marinak

Akkorra már belepték a legyek

túl az agónián
túl a tetanuszon,
és messze túl szögeken, sebeken
se tárgy, se test
nyilvánosan
között
se ácsorgás
(behorpadt szentségtartó),
se röpülés

barát,
barátság mindörökre.

HOLY THIEF

For Mari Törőcsik

By then the flies had covered him

beyond agony,
beyond tetanus,
and far beyond nails, wounds,
neither object nor body,
in public
in between
neither loitering
(dented monstrance)
nor flight

friend,
friendship forever.

from *Splinters* (1972)

AMIKÉNT KEZDTEM

Amiként kezdtem, végig az maradtam.
Ahogyan kezdtem, mindvégig azt csinálom.
Mint a fegyenc, ki visszatérve
falujába, továbbra is csak hallgat,
szótlanul űl pohár bora előtt.

AS I BEGAN

As I began, so I remained to the end.
What I began, that's what I do to the finish.
Like the convict who, returning
to his village, keeps on being silent,
sits wordless before his glass of wine.

JUTTÁNAK

Levél

Veled együtt es velem együtt
az idő minden ütése-kopása
és erőssége hó alá kerül
abban a végső feledésben,
amit az Atya küld majd a világra.

Január

A tél növekszik.
Egy magányos farkas jött le a faluba.
Reszket előtted.
Mise ez.
Utolsó áldozás.

Naplórészlet

Milyen nap is van ma? Úgy élek,
hogy össze-összezavarom
az idő menetrendjét.
"Latrokként − Simone Weil gyönyörű szavával
− tér és idő keresztjére
vagyunk mi verve emberek."
Elalélok, és a szálkák fölriasztanak.
Ilyenkor metsző élességgel látom a világot,
és megpróbálom feléd fordítani a fejemet.

FOR JUTTA

Letter

Together with you and together with me,
time's every bruise, scuff-mark,
and strength gets buried under snow
in that final oblivion
that the Father will send upon the world.

January

Winter is growing.
A lonely wolf came down into the village.
He is trembling before you.
This is Mass.
Final Communion.

Fragment from a Diary

What day did you say this was? I live
so that I mix and shuffle
time's bus schedule.
"Like thieves," in the beautiful words of Simone Weil,
"we humans are crucified
on the cross of time and space." I doze off
and the splinters startle me into wakefulness.
At such times I see the world with cutting sharpness,
and try to turn my head toward you.

A MÉLYPONT ÜNNEPÉLYE

Az ólak véres melegében
ki mer olvasni?
És ki mer
a lemenő nap szálkamezejében,
az ég dagálya és
a föld apálya idején
útrakelni, akárhová?

Ki mer
csukott szemmel megállani
ama mélyponton,
ott, ahol
mindíg akad egy utolsó legyintés,
háztető,
gyönyörü arc, vagy akár
egyetlen kéz, fejbólintás, kézmozdulat?

Ki tud
nyugodt szívvel belesimúlni
az álomba, mely túlcsap a gyerekkor
keservein s a tengert
marék vízként arcához emeli?

CELEBRATION OF NADIR

In the bloodstained warmth of the barns
who dare read?
And who dare,
in the splinter-meadow of the setting sun,
at a time of sky-tide
and earth-ebb,
set out on a journey, anywhere?

Who dare
stop with eyes closed
at that nadir,
there, where there's always
one last wave of the hand left,
a roof,
beautiful face or, for that matter,
a single hand, head-nod, gesture?

Who can
smoothly slip with tranquil heart
into dream that surfbreaks beyond childhood's
sorrows and lifts the sea,
like a handful of water, to its face?

A HÓHÉR SZOBÁJA

Szalonnaszag. Muskátliszag.
Tengert sose látni a hóhér szobájának ablakából.
A tenger Istené,
s az ablak csukva van.

Milyen más a vesztőhely illata,
és a bárány, amikor értejönnek.

THE HENCHMAN'S ROOM

Bacon smell. Geranium smell.
You never see the sea from the window of the henchman's room.
The sea belongs to God,
and the window is closed.

How different the fragrance of the gallows,
and the lamb, when they come for him.

BŰN ÉS BŰNHŐDÉS

Sheryl Suttonnak

A befalazott képzelet
még egyre ismételgeti –

A pillanat villanyszék trónusán
még ott az arc,
sziklába mártott nyakszirt,
gyönyörü kéz –
pórusos jelenléted.

Még tart a nyár.

Ereszd le jogarod, királynő.

CRIME AND PUNISHMENT

For Sheryl Sutton

Walled-up imagination
keeps on repeating:

On the moment's electric-chair throne,
there it is still: the face,
the scruff dipped in rock,
the beautiful hand—
your porous presence.

It's still summer.

Lower your scepter, Queen.

ÖRÖKMOZGÓ

A világbank elektromos szivében
az örökmozgó föl-lejár,
mint egy tükör,
mint egy koporsó,
mozgókép, vitrin, üveghintó,
akár egy óriási mécses,
holtfáradt, óriás kisértet.

PERPETUUM MOBILE

In the World Bank's electric heart,
the perpetuum mobile goes up and down,
like a mirror,
like a coffin,
a motion picture, vitrine, glass coach,
just like an enormous oil lamp,
a dead tired, gigantic ghost.

METRONÓM

Mérd az időt,
de ne a mi időnket,
a szálkák mozdulatlan jelenét,
a fölvonóhíd fokait,
a téli vesztőhely havát,
ösvények és tisztások csöndjét,
a töredék foglalatában
az Atyaisten ígéretét.

METRONOME

Measure time,
but not our time,
the splinters' motionless present,
the degrees of the drawbridge,
the winter gallows' snow,
silence of footpaths and clearings,
in the fragment's jewel setting
the promise of God the Father.

INTELEM

Ne a lélekzetvételt. A zihálást.
Ne a nászasztalt. A lehulló
maradékot, hideget, árnyakat.
Ne a mozdulatot. A kapkodást.
A kampó csöndjét, azt jegyezd.

Arra figyelj, amire városod,
az örök város máig is figyel:
tornyaival, tetőivel,
élő és halott polgáraival.

Akkor talán még napjaidban
hírül adhatod azt, miről
hírt adnod itt egyedűl érdemes.

Írnok,
akkor talán nem jártál itt hiába.

ADMONITION

Not breathing. Panting.
Not the wedding table. The falling
scraps, the cold, the shadows.
Not movement. Clutching at straws.
The hook's silence: note that.

Mind what your city,
the eternal city minds to this day:
with its towers, roofs,
its citizens living and dead.

Then perhaps in your lifetime still
you may release as news
what alone is worth your while releasing.

Scribe:
then perhaps you will not have been here in vain.

VESZTŐHELY TÉLEN

Kit fölvezetnek?   Nem tudom.
Kik fölvezetik?   Nem tudom.
Vágóhíd vagy vesztőhely?   Nem tudom.
Ki es kit öl? Ember öl állatot
vagy állat embert?   Nem tudom.
S a zuhanás, a félreérthetetlen,
s a csönd utána?   Nem tudom.
S a hó, a téli hó? Talán
száműzött tenger, Isten hallgatása.

Vesztőhely télen. Semmit sem tudunk.

GALLOWS IN WINTER

Whom they lead up?	I don't know.
Who lead him up?	I don't know.
Is it a stockyard or a gallows?	I don't know.
Who kills and whom? Does man kill beast,	
or beast man?	I don't know.
And the plunging, not to be misunderstood,	
and the silence after that?	I don't know.
And the snow, the winter snow? Perhaps	
an exiled sea, God's silence.	

Gallows in winter. We know nothing.

VAN GOGH IMÁJA

Csatavesztés a földeken.
Honfoglalás a levegőben.
Madarak, nap és megint madarak.
Estére mi marad belőlem?

Estére csak a lámpasor,
a sárga vályogfal ragyog,
s a kert alól, a fákon át,
mint gyertyasor, az ablakok;

hol én is laktam, s nem lakom,
a ház, hol éltem, és nem élek,
a tető, amely betakart.
Istenem, betakartál régen.

VAN GOGH'S PRAYER

Rout in battle in the fields.
Settling of the homeland in air.
Birds, sun, and again birds.
What's left of me by evening?

By evening only the row of lamps,
the yellow mud wall glisten,
and from the garden, through the trees,
like a row of candles, the windows;

where I too dwelled, and do not dwell,
the house where I lived, and do not live,
the roof that covered me.
My God, you covered me long ago.

MINDEN LÉLEKZETVÉTEL

Minden lélekzetvétel megsebez,
és leterít valahány szívverés.
Különös, hogy a tenger halhatatlan,
holott minden hulláma végitélet.

Hogyan is igazítja sorsát,
az öröklétet, Isten, a teremtés
mindörökre veszendő mezejében?

Mint a füvek lemondó élete,
mint a halandók egy-egy szívütése,
olyan lehet végülis a dicsőség,
Isten nyugalmas boldogsága.

EVERY BREATH

Each breath wounds me,
and every single heartbeat lays me low.
Strange that the sea should be deathless,
when its every wave is a doomsday judgment.

Just how does he direct his fate,
eternal being, God, in creation's
eternally death-marked field?

Like the resigned life of grasses,
like this or that heartbeat of mortals,
that's how glory must be in the end,
God's tranquil happiness.

A TÖBBI KEGYELEM

A félelem s az álom
volt apám és anyám.
A folyosó meg a
kitáruló vidék.

Így éltem. Hogy halok meg?
Milyen lesz pusztulásom?

A föld elárúl. Magához ölel.
A többi kegyelem.

THE REST IS MERCY

Fear and dream
were my father and my mother.
The corridor and the
opening land.

This is how I lived. How will I die?
What will my dissolution be like?

Earth will betray me. It will hug me to itself.
The rest is mercy.

TALÁLKOZÁSOK

Szilágyi Júliának

Hányféle találkozás, Istenem,
együttlét, különválás, búcsuzás!
Hullám hullámmal, virág a virágtól
szélcsendben, szélben
mozdúlva, mozdulatlan úl
hány és hányféle színeváltozás,
a múlandó s a múlhatatlan
hányféle helycseréje!

MEETINGS

For Júlia Szilágyi

Meetings of how many different kinds, dear God!
togetherness, separation, farewell!
Wave with wave, flower from flower
in windless calm, moving in
wind, motionless;
how many changes of color, and of how many kinds;
all the different changes of place
between what will pass and what stays!

A POKOL HETEDIK KÖRE

A pokol első, második,
harmadik, negyedik köre,
majd az ötödik, hatodik
és végül is a legutolsó.

Itthon vagyok.
Engedd, hogy lepihenjek
és meggörbűlve elaludjak végre,
hiszen itt is jelen vagy.

THE SEVENTH CIRCLE OF HELL

Hell's first, second,
third, fourth circle,
then the fifth, sixth
and, at long last, the very last one.

I am home.
Let me lie down to rest
and, curling up, go to sleep at last;
here too you are present, after all.

EGY ÉLETEN KERESZTŰL

Sógorom emlékezetére

1.

Mi törjük el, repesztjük ketté,
mi egyedűl és mi magunk
azt, ami egy és oszthatatlan.

2.

Utána azután
egy hosszú-hosszú életen keresztűl
próbáljuk vakon, süketen, hiába
összefércelni a világ
makulátlan és eredendő szövetét.

3.

Gyerekkorunkban meg kellene halnunk,
tudásunk csúcsán, alázatunk magasán,
de tovább élünk, foltozgatva és
tóldozgatva a jóvátehetetlent.

4.

Még jó, hogy elalhatunk közbe-közbe
és utóljára.

THROUGH A LIFETIME

In memory of my brother-in-law

1.

We are the ones who break, crack in two,
we alone and we ourselves,
what is one and indivisible.

2.

Then afterwards,
through a long, long life,
we try, blind, deaf, in vain,
to mend the world's
immaculate and primeval cloth.

3.

We should by rights die in our childhoods,
on the pinnacle of our knowledge, at the height of our humility,
but we go on living, patching and
repairing the irreparable.

4.

It's good we can go to sleep off and on
and for the last time.

A TÉKOZLÓ FIÚ KERESÉSE

Itt lakott kétségtelenűl.
Látod? Látom.
A mi fiúnk.
Űlj az ablakba, nézd a házakat,
aztán a szobát, falakat,
a jégveremnél hidegebb
éléskamrát, mosdóhelyet.
Most pedig indúljunk haza.

LOOKING FOR THE PRODIGAL SON

Here he lived without a doubt.
Do you see him? I see him.
Our son.
Sit in the window, look at the houses,
then the room, the walls,
the larder, lavatory,
colder than an ice pit.
And now let's set out for home.

MARHABÉLYEG

1.

Nincs az a marhabélyeg,
mit meg ne érdemelnék.

Jó lesz átlépnem a halál
fehérre meszelt küszöbét.

Minden jó, amit megérdemeltünk.

2.

A világ tenyerébe kalapált szeg,
holtsápadt,
csurom vér vagyok.

CATTLE BRAND

1.

There is no cattle brand
that I don't deserve.

I had better cross death's
whitewashed threshold.

All that we have deserved is good.

2.

Nail hammered into the world's palm,
I'm deathly pale.
Blooddrenched.

AHOGYAN CSAK

Esti mise, téli vecsernye,
éjféli Úrfölmutatás,
miként a hó hallgat a meglepett
fák alján, ahogyan csupán
téli égbolt erős, szilárd,
úgy vérzenek jók, rosszak együtt,
bárányok, füvek, farkasok
halálunk monstranciájában.

THE WAY ONLY

Evening Mass, winter evensong,
midnight elevation of the Host,
the way snow keeps silent at the bases
of surprised trees, the way only a
winter sky is strong, solid,
that's how the good and the bad bleed together,
lambs, grasses, wolves,
in our death's monstrance.

ELÉG

A teremtés bármilyen széles,
ólnál is szűkösebb.
Innét odáig. Kő, fa, ház.
Teszek, veszek. Korán jövök, megkésem.

És mégis olykor belép valaki
és ami van, hirtelenül kitárúl.
Elég egy arc látványa, egy jelenlét,
s a tapéták vérezni kezdenek.

Elég, igen, egy kéz elég amint
megkeveri a kávét, vagy ahogy
"visszavonúl a bemutatkozásból",
elég, hogy elfeledjük a helyet,
a levegőtlen ablaksort, igen,
hogy visszatérve éjszaka szobánkba
elfogadjuk az elfogadhatatlant.

ENOUGH

However spacious creation,
it is more cramped than a pigpen.
Here to there. Stone, tree, house.
I putter. I come early, arrive late.

And yet at times someone steps in,
and what exists, suddenly flies open.
The sight of a face, a presence is enough,
and the wallpaper starts in bleeding.

Yes, that will do: a hand will, as it
stirs the coffee, or as it
"pulls back from the introduction";
it's enough that we forget the spot,
the airless row of windows, yes;
that, returning to our rooms at night,
we should accept the unacceptable.

EGYENES LABIRINTUS

Milyen lesz az a visszaröpülés,
amiről csak hasonlatok beszélnek,
olyanfélék, hogy oltár, szentély,
kézfogás, visszatérés, ölelés,
fűben, fák alatt megterített asztal,
hol nincs első és nincs utolsó vendég,
végül is milyen lesz, milyen lesz
e nyitott szárnyú emelkedő zuhanás,
visszahullás a fókusz lángoló
közös fészkébe? – nem tudom,
és mégis, hogyha valamit tudok,
hát ezt tudom, e forró folyosót,
e nyílegyenes labirintust, melyben
mind tömöttebb és mind tömöttebb
és egyre szabadabb a tény, hogy röpülünk.

STRAIGHT LABYRINTH

What will it be like—that return flight
of which only metaphors speak,
such as: altar, sanctuary,
handshake, return, embrace,
in grass, under trees, a set table
where there is no first and no last guest;
how, how in the end will this be, this
open-winged, lifting plunging,
this falling-back into focus's flaming,
shared nest?—I don't know,
and yet if there is anything I know,
well—I know this, this hot corridor,
this arrow-straight labyrinth, in which it's
increasingly closer, denser, and
constantly freer—the fact that we're flying.

from *Dénouement* (1974)

KÉT ARCKÉP

Marinak és Gyuszinak

Brontë

A kocsisok beüzennek: jövünk.
És a vendégek: érkezünk.
És a lámpások átszelik
röpködve a teret, az udvart,
fénybe vonva az éjszakát,
a diófák törzsét, a szőlők
alsószoknyáját s a kőasztal
esőbe-szélbe mártott peremét.

Hát itt vagyunk.
Nyissatok ajtót.
Ez az utolsó éjszakánk.
Ez az utolsó vendégségünk.

Terítsetek.
Ágyazzatok.
Rakjátok meg a kályhát.
Eresszétek szabadon a kutyákat.

Rembrandt

Atyai ház: hamuból és ecetből.
Csók és kézcsók: hamuból és ecetből.
Csukott szemek a sírban és az ágyban,
halálon túli fegyelemben.

TWO PORTRAITS

For Mari and Gyuszi

Brontë

The coachmen send in word: we're coming.
And the guests: we're arriving.
And, fluttering, the lanterns
slice through square and courtyard,
gilding with light the night,
the walnuts' trunks, the vines'
petticoats, and the stone table's
rain- and wind-dipped rim.

So then—we're here.
Open the door.
This is our final night.
This is our last visit.

Set the table.
Make the bed.
Stack the stove.
Let the dogs loose.

Rembrandt

Paternal house: of ashes and vinegar.
Kiss and handkiss: of ashes and vinegar.
Eyes closed in grave and in bed,
in a discipline beyond death.

157

NYITÁS

A gyerekkor alkímiája
beteljesűl, sikerűl végre.
Az érintetlen kapukat,
az álom zsiliprendszer ét kinyitják.
Mindenből csönd lesz és közelség.

OPENING

Childhood's alchemy
fulfilled, a success at last.
They open the untouched gates,
the sluice-system of dream.
All becomes silence and closeness.

JÁTSZMA

A zöldposztós asztalra hajlik
halott apám.
De mi fölé hajol?
És mit akar, mit is akar,
és mit is mond e kivilágított,
besüppedt sír,
magányos játszma,
férfihát?

Ne zavarjuk, ne zavarjátok
előretartott jobb és hátravont
bal kézfejét, s a dákó
három golyó közt fölfüggesztett
figyelmét, részarányosát.

Hiszen,
a golyó és a dákó elsötétül,
nélkületek, nélkülem is megáll,
és velük együtt én is, akiért
e játszma zajlik
egyszer s mindenkorra.

GAME

Leaning over the green felt-covered table
it's my dead father.
But what is it that he leans over?
And what, just what does it intend;
what is this lit-up,
caved-in gravesite,
this solitary game, this
man-back saying?

Let us not, don't you, disturb the backs
of his held-out right and drawn-back
left hand, and the cue's
attentiveness, ratio, suspended
among three balls.

After all,
ball and cue darken,
halt, even without you, without me,
and with them I too halt, for whom
this game now clatters on,
once, and forever.

MEGHATÁROZÁS

Féregnek lenni mit jelent?
Vágyakozni egy tekintetre,
egy olyan hosszú, nyílt szembesülésre,
ahogy csak Isten nézi önmagát,
erre vágyni, egyedül erre,
és ugyanakkor üveges szemekkel
belefuródni abba, ami nincs,
beszorúlva a semmi és
valamiféle utánzat közé.

DEFINITION

To be a worm: what does that mean?
To crave a glance,
an eye-to-eye meeting as prolonged, as open
as only God gazes on himself;
to long for this, for this alone,
and at the same time to burrow
with glassy eyes into what is not,
squeezed between nothing and
some sort of imitation.

TAPASZTALAT

A tapasztalat, mint Kronosz
fölfalja fiait.
A valódi tudás
tapasztalatlan, mit se tud,
nem ismer, nem ismerhet semmit.

Így érez, így érezhet egyedűl
örök békét, nyugalmat, amikor
a hóhér szalonnázik, s ő maga
gyanútlanul megérkezik, belép,
majd megfeszűl, hátrahanyatlik,
s vérezni kezd egy nem létező térben,
amihez csak a mennyország hasonló.

EXPERIENCE

Experience, like Kronos,
eats his sons.
Genuine knowledge
is inexperienced, knows nothing,
is acquainted, can be acquainted with nothing.

So he feels, so only can he feel
eternal peace, calm, when
the henchman snacks on bacon, and he himself
unsuspectingly arrives, steps in,
then stiffens, lies down supine,
and starts bleeding in a nonexistent space
that only heaven resembles.

SZTAVROGIN ELKÖSZÖN

"Unatkozom. Kérem a köpenyem.
Mielőtt bármit elkövetnek,
gondoljanak a rózsakertre,
vagy még inkább egyetlen rózsatőre,
egyetlen egy rózsára, uraim."

STAVROGIN SAYS GOODBYE

"I am bored. My robe, please.
Before you commit any act,
think of the rose garden,
sooner yet, of a single rose tree,
of a single rose, gentlemen."

ÉKSZER

Remekbe készült, ovális tükörben
nézi magát az antilop.
Nyakában drágakő.

Azt mondjuk rá, szép, mint egy faliszőnyeg.
Azt mondjuk neki, te csak nézd magad,
mi majd szülünk, születünk, meghalunk.

Ilyesféléket susogunk neki,
az őrületben élő antilopnak.

JEWEL

In a masterly crafted oval mirror
the antelope looks at herself.
About her neck a precious stone.

We say of her, She is beautiful as a tapestry.
We say to her, You just be looking at yourself;
we'll be giving birth, we'll be born, we'll die.

That's the sort of thing we whisper into her ear,
of the antelope, living in delirium.

GYÓNÁS UTÁN

Bevallottam: *a naplementét Svájcban.*
Nem lett volna szabad.
Gonosz féreg az önvád. Az erősek
hajnalban kelnek, fát aprítanak,
isznak egy korty pálinkát, s így tovább.
Mivel csak ők, az erős gyilkosok
ismerik a füvek, fák, madarak,
a nők és a csecsemők nyelvét.

AFTER CONFESSION

I confessed: *to sunset in Switzerland.*
I shouldn't have done it.
A wicked worm, self-accusation. The strong
rise at dawn, chop wood,
drink a gulp of brandy, and so on.
Since only they, the strong murderers,
know the language of grasses, trees, birds,
the language of women and of infants.

INFINITÍVUSZ

Még ki lehet nyitni.
És be lehet zárni.
Még föl lehet kötni.
És le lehet vágni.
Még meg lehet szülni.
És el lehet ásni.

INFINITIVE   ·

It's still possible to open it.
And to lock him in.
It's still possible to string him up.
And to cut him down.
It's still possible to give him birth.
And to shovel him under.

KÖLTEMÉNY

Nem föld a föld.
Nem szám a szám.
Nem betű a betű.
Nem mondat a mondat.

Isten az Isten.
Virág a virág.
Daganat a daganat.
Tél a tél.
Gyűjtőtábor a körülhatárolt
bizonytalan formájú terület.

POEM

Earth is not earth.
Number is not number.
Letter is not letter.
Sentence is no sentence.

God is God.
A flower is a flower.
A swelling is a swelling.
Winter is winter.
The fenced-in area of indefinite shape
is a concentration camp.

SZTAVROGIN VISSZATÉR

"Nem gondoltak a rózsakertre,
és elkövették, amit nem szabad.

Ezentúl üldözöttek lesznek
és magányosak, mint egy lepkegyűjtő.
Üveg alá kerülnek valahányan.

Üveg alatt, tűhegyre szúrva
ragyog, ragyog a lepketábor.
Önök ragyognak, uraim.

Félek. Kérem a köpenyem."

STAVROGIN RETURNS

"You did not think of the rose garden,
and committed what is forbidden.

"From now on you'll be hunted,
and lonely, like a butterfly collector.
You'll go under glass, every last one of you.

"Under glass, mounted on pins,
the encampment of butterflies glisten, glisten.
It's you who glisten, gentlemen.

"I am frightened. My robe, please."

from *Crater* (1976)

AUSCHWITZ

Schaár Erzsébetnek

Négy-öt esztendős lehetek,
s az én koromban a világ,
vagy – ha úgy tetszik – a valóság,
egyszóval mindaz, ami van,
két esztendő vagy nyolcvan év,
mázsás cipő, több tonnás kiskabát,
és főként, ami hátra van még,
pontosan öt-hat éves.

AUSCHWITZ

For Erzsébet Schaár

I could be four, five years old,
and at my age the world,
or—if you please—reality,
in a word, all there is,
two years or eighty,
hundredweight shoe, jacket weighing several tons,
and especially all that's still to come,
is exactly five, six years old.

TEREK

A pokol térélmény. A mennyország is.
Kétféle tér. A mennyország szabad,
a másikra lefele látunk,
mint egy alagsori szobába,
föntről lefele látunk, mintha
egy lépcsőházból kukucskálnánk lefele
egy akarattal nyitva hagyott (felejtett?)
alagsori szobának ajtaján át.
Ott az történik, ami épp nekem
kibírhatatlan. Talán nem egyéb,
kibontanak egy rongyosládát,
lemérik, hány kiló egy hattyú,
vagy ezerszeres ismétlésben
olyasmiről beszélnek azzal
az egyetlen lénnyel, kit szeretek,
miről se írni, se beszélni
nem lehet, nem szabad.

SPACES

Hell is an experience of space. So is heaven.
Two kinds of space. Heaven is wide open;
into the other we see downward,
as into a room in the basement:
we see from the top downward, as if
we were peeking down from a stairwell
through the door of a basement room
left open on purpose (forgotten?).
What goes on there is what I of all people
find unbearable. Perhaps it's nothing other than
that they pry open a rag chest,
they weigh a swan—how many kilograms?—
or that in thousandfold repetition
they speak, with that
sole being whom I love,
about matters about which we can, we must
neither write nor speak.

ÁLOM

A nemtelen lény lehajol,
lehajol, s fölemelkedik.
Szépsége feleslegesebb
és fontosabb egy elnökválasztásnál.

Sárga haját megérinti a szél,
szövetséget kötök vele,
a gyönyörű fej elgondolkodik,
s úgy néz szembe, hogy nem látni szemét.

DREAM

The genderless being bends down,
bends down, and straightens.
Its beauty is more superfluous
and more important than a presidential election.

The wind touches its flaxen hair;
I make a pact with it;
the beautiful head becomes absorbed in thought,
and looks straight at me so that you cannot see its eyes.

KETTŐ

Két fehér súly figyeli egymást,
két hófehér és vaksötét súly.
Vagyok, mert nem vagyok.

TWO

Two white weights are watching each other,
two snowwhite and blinding dark weights.
I am because I am not.

HÖLDERLIN

Kurtág Györgynek

December hője, nyarak jégverése,
drótvégre csomózott madár,
mi nem voltam én? Boldogan halok.

HÖLDERLIN

For György Kurtág

Heat of December, hailstorm of summers,
bird knotted to the end of wire,
what have I not been? Gladly I'll die.

ZÖLD

Elmerűl szemem, arcom, lelkem,
minden élőlény megmerűl
abban a feneketlen zöldben,
ami egy fa kívűl-belűl.

GREEN

My eyes, face, soul founder,
all living beings are immersed
in that fathomless green
that a tree is, inside and out.

KŐEDÉNY

Ember, állat egyként pulzál szivemben.
Mint kőedényen a piros máz,
úgy ég rajtam a csorgó, foltos
és közös veriték.

EARTHEN VESSEL

Man, beast pulse in my heart as one.
As on an earthen vessel the red glaze,
so it burns on me: the dripping, staining,
and shared perspiration.

GÓTIKA

A csúszó-mászó, belefeledkezve
vállra omló hajadba, figyeli
romolhatatlan, veszendő tökélyed.

A senki néz.
A semmi néz.
Az ízeltlábú nézi a napot.
A tört, a gyűrt, a szaggatott
a kereket, lángolót, mozdulatlant.

Most minden egy. Együtt van. Egybeolvad.
A mindenség modellje, áll a templom.

GOTHIC

The creeper-crawler, under the spell
of your shoulder-cascading hair, watches
your incorruptible, doomed perfection.

The no one looks at you.
The nothing looks at you.
The arthropod looks at the sun.
What is broken, wrinkled, torn,
at the wheel, the flaming, unmoving one.

Now all is one. Together. Melts into one.
As a model of the All, stands the church.

KRÁTER

Találkoztunk. Találkozunk.
Egy trafikban. Egy árverésen.
Keresgéltél valamit. Elmozdítasz
valamit. Menekülnék. Maradok.
Cigarettára gyújtok. Távozol.

Leszállsz és fölszállsz.
Fölszállok és leszállok.
Cigaretta. Lépkedel. Lépkedek.
Egyhelyben járunk; mint a gyilkos
a járásodban gázolok.

Madárcsicsergés ahogyan
szememre veted születésem.
Azt, hogy itt állunk. Majd egy útszakasz
holtágában a motyogásom
gurulni kezd, legördűl óriás
tagjaidról és ama diadalmas
és vakító valamiről,
ami már nem te vagy.

Úgy érint elutasításod,
ez a parázna, kőbeírott suhintás,
hogy tekintetem – két kavics –
azóta is csak gurul és gurul
egy hófehér kráterben. Két szemem,
ket szem pattog: az üdvösségem.

CRATER

We've met. We go on meeting.
In a cigar store. At an auction.
You were rummaging for something. You're dislodging
something. I'd like to flee. I'm staying.
I light up a cigarette. You're leaving.

You get off and get on.
I get on and get off.
Cigarette. You're pacing. I'm pacing.
We walk in the same spot; like a murderer,
I tailgate you as you walk.

It's bird-twitter, the way
you reproach me for my birth.
For our standing here. Then, in the cul-de-sac
of a leg of the journey, my mutter
starts in rolling, pearls off your enormous
limbs and off that triumphant
and blinding something
that is not you any more.

Your snub, this licentious
whisk, written in stone, has touched me
so that my glance—two pebbles—has
just been rolling and rolling since
in a snow-white crater. My two eyes,
two eyes sputter: my salvation.

B. I. KISASSZONY

Küldj fésüt és konzervet.
A régi fésü, szóval, eltörött.

Küldj cipőt. Meleg alsót.
Képzeld, úgy hivnak, Vasgolyó.
Még három év. A kert vacak.

Vigyázz, hogy ne kerülj ide.
Bár a karácsony szebb, mint otthon.
De két golyó, mondjuk, hogy összekoccan.
Az is mi? Nincsen folytatása.

Holnap vagyok itt utoljára.
Kezet csókoltam mindenkinek.
Más okból voltam én itt. Fedő bűnnel
sikerült eltakarnom azt az igazit,.
azt, amit nem, nem, nem lehet
se elviselni, se kimondani.

Bűn az, minek nyomát is
sikerül eltüntetnünk.

Holnaptól ellenállás nélkül,
egyenletesen gurulok.

MISS I. B.

Send me a comb and canned goods.
The old comb broke, in a word.

Send shoes. Warm undies.
Imagine, they call me Iron Ball.
Three more years. The garden is lousy.

Watch it, so you don't wind up here.
Though Christmas is nicer than back home.
But two balls, let's say, gently colliding.
What's that, anyway? It doesn't continue.

Tomorrow I'm here for the last time.
I kissed everybody's hand.
I was here for other cause. With a cover-up crime
I succeeded in shielding that real one,
the one you can't, can't, simply cannot
either bear or say out loud.

Crime is what we succeed in
removing the very trace of.

Starting tomorrow, without resistance,
evenly: I'm rolling.

VÁZLAT

Üss le. A bajuszod tovább nő,
nekem viszont van egy-két oly emlékem,
hogy pontosan tudom a különbséget
a természetes testmeleg
és a szerelem melege között.

Pedig én csak öt éves voltam,
s a lány tizenhat.

A legcsodásabb az, hogy két meleg
tudhat egymásról; mai szóval,
milliárd közlés lehetséges
két test között,
anélkül, hogy találkoznának.

Micsicsák rabruhát viselt,
én habos gallért és bársony ruhácskát.
Ő elpusztult, én pusztulok.

SKETCH

Strike me dead. Your moustache keeps on growing,
while I have a memory or two
to tell me the exact difference
between natural body heat
and the heat of love.

Though I was only five,
and the girl sixteen.

The most marvelous part is that two warmths
can know of each other; in today's parlance,
a billion communications are possible
between two bodies
without their meeting.

Micsicsák wore a prison garment,
I a frilled collar and a little velvet outfit.
She perished; I'm perishing.

NOTES ON THE POEMS

In the following notes, every effort has been made to identify persons and other allusions in the poems, and to cite the poet's important debts and affinities. As in the notes to the Introduction, abbreviated citations refer to entries present in the Bibliography. Following the title of a poem and double page citations (to *CP* and to the present selection), A: indicates the first appearance of a given poem, as shown in the table of contents of *CP* (243-52). These data complete where possible those compiled by István Jelenits. An asterisk following a citation means that the poem originally appeared in a form somewhat different from that in which *CP* prints it. In the notes "line," "stanza," and "section" are written out, except for section 1, line 1, which is cited in the form 1.1. For "KZ Oratorio" only, citation is by page and line (62, 12; 77, 22 [here, every printed line is counted]). Poems cited by *CP* only are not translated in the present selection.

from *Trapeze and Parallel Bars* (1946)

"Under a Winter Sky" (17-18; 5)
A: *Ezüstkor* (Silver Age) 1, no. 1 (March 1943): 70.
Dedicatee: Tamás Cholnoky: a secure identification could not be obtained. In a letter Dr. Péter Kovács, the poet's nephew and the present heir to his literary rights, tells me that he seems to recall TCh from early years.

Lines 3-4 "I lean / supine against the wall": gesture of leaning; cf. "KZ Oratorio" 61, 16; 75, 21.

Line 16 "no god will protect me": Tüskés (75) states that "most probably at the editors' request" the line in its magazine appearance was altered to read: "not suffering, not torment!" Restored, it tells of agnosticism, the sense of an absent God, which even at this early stage JP shares with Hölderlin, the author of the ode "Dichterberuf" and the elegy "Brod und Wein." See Friedrich

Hölderlin, *Sämtliche Werke und Briefe*, ed. Michael Knaupp, 3 vols. (Munich: Carl Hanser, 1992), 1:329-31 ("Dichterberuf," second version), 1:372-82 (left-hand pages only: "Brod und Wein," first version). Cited as Hanser, volume, and page. On JP's affinity with the German poet, see also the notes on "Apocrypha" and "Hölderlin."

Lines 19-20: To understand these lines Revelation, one of JP's favorite books of the Bible, seems quite enough. Yet there seems to be some affinity with the closing lines of W. B. Yeats's "The Second Coming"; for text, see *The Variorum Edition of the Poems of W. B. Yeats*, ed. Peter Allt and Russell K. Alspach (New York: Macmillan, 1957, ²1965) 401-02, especially lines 13-16, 21-22. The resemblance cannot be read as a case of influence, since JP knew no English. In later years he may well have known the translation of Yeats's poem by László Nagy; see Nagy László, *Versek és versfordítások* (Poems and Translations), 3 vols., 2nd ed. rev. and enl. (Budapest: Magvető, 1978) 2:142-43. LN's translations appeared in book form in 1975 (*KMÍK*). For an indication of JP's awareness of LN, see *Nadir* 1:491 (short obit in *Új Ember* dated 19 February 1978).

With the Revelation motif in the two closing lines, cf. below, "Revelation 8:7" and "Apocrypha," and the notes on these poems.

"Belated Grace" (19; 7)

A: *Budapest* 2, no. 12 (December 1946): 449.

Opening stanza: S. Radnóti (85) connects it with Prince Myshkin's (no doubt autobiographical) tale of the condemned man pardoned in the shadow of the gallows; see Fedor Dostoevsky, *The Idiot*, trans. Alan Myers, with an Introduction by William Leatherbarrow, The World's Classics (Oxford, New York: Oxford UP, 1992) 22-23; 23. Cited as Oxford and page.

Line 11 "his mother": important for JP as material for poetry; cf. "Példabeszéd" ("Parable") (*CP* 91); "Mégis nehéz" ("Still It's Difficult") (*CP* 107); certainly JP's first published and as yet uncollected poem "Anyám" ("My Mother") (*CP* 147).

Line 16 "a perishing world": JP's vision is one conditioned not merely by a specific historic event, however apocalyptic, but also by our continuous process of dying. Cf. the closing line of "Sketch."

"Because You Were Soaking Wet, Were Cold" (19-20; 9)
A: *Magyarok* (Hungarians) 2, nos. 2-3 (February-March 1946): 73.
Dedicatee: György Rónay (1913-1978), poet, essayist, novelist, anthologist, diarist, leading liberal Catholic intellectual, JP's mentor and friend. On the spiritual affinities between the two writers, see Hegyi. See also Rónay, *Diaries*, especially the entries for 4 June 1952 (1:522), 9 September 1952 (1:621-22), 27 August 1955 (2:416), and 29 September 1957 (2:552).

Line 2 "monsters lying in wait": cf. "Under a Winter Sky," line 20.

Line 14 "in me": see Tandori, 1983, 359-60.

Line 18 "stammering noise": faint but audible allusion to Bébi and to JP's second wife, Ingrid Fichieux (Tüskés 24-26, 282).

Lines 9-12, 23-24: unmistakable Magrittean effects, although by the time JP wrote these lines he would probably not have seen works by the Belgian surrealist painter (on René Magritte, see also the notes on "To Two Lovers," "Metropolitan Icons," and "The Henchman's Room").

from *On the Third Day* (1959)

"Paraphrase" (27-28; 13-15)
A: *Újhold* (New Moon) 1, no. 2 (December 1946): 82, as "Eleven étketek
   vagyok" ("I Am Your Living Food") *
Comment: Tandori, 1983, 360.

Lines 1-4, notions of anthropophagy: cf. "French Prisoner" and the note there; also S. Radnóti 96-97 (juxtaposes a quotation from the poem with one from the early "Halak a hálóban" ["Fish in a Net"] [*CP* 11]).

Lines 7-8, image of frustrated or hostile love: cf. "Love's Desert," and note.

Lines 13 "trough," 14 "feeder": suggestion of the degradation of humans to hogs and other farm animals; the passage resonates with "Harbach 1944," "Frankfurt," "KZ Oratorio" (66, 11-12; 87, 15-16), and with the theme of the Prodigal Son, as treated in "Looking for the Prodigal Son." See especially the note on lines 3-5 of this last-named poem.

"Without Witnesses" (30-31; 17)
A: *Magyarok* 3, no. 8 (August 1947): 38. *
Title: Witness motif, cf. "On a KZ Lager's Wall," line 12 "you testify against us." In tone and imagery, the poem presages both "On a KZ Lager's Wall" and "Ravensbrück Passion."

Line 1 "outlined against the world": A Paul Klee-like formulation. JP did not see works by Klee until he visited Switzerland (Berne) in the fall and winter of 1965 (on Klee, see *Nadir* 1:295-96; article dated 25 December 1965).

Lines 3-4 "hell" and how it works on the poet: cf. "The Seventh Circle of Hell" and "Spaces."

Lines 15-16 "the henchman's / basket": on "henchman," cf. "From the Henchman's Diary," "The Henchman's Room," "Experience," and the notes there. On "basket": the image of the guillotine is prominent in Prince Myshkin's discourse on the condemned and then pardoned man (Oxford 22-23; see also above, note on "Belated Grace").

"To Two Lovers" (31; 19)
A: *Vigilia* 14, no. 2 (February 1949): 97.

Line 13, worm motif: cf. "Paraphrase," "Definition," also "In memoriam N. N." (*CP* 31-32), lines 21-22, 34.

Line 20 "an enormous infant": Magrittean effect. See Jacques Meuris, *Magritte* (n.p. [Paris]: Nouvelles Éditions Françaises, 1988), fig. 237, *La Chambre d'Écoute* (full color plate, half page, showing green apple occupying entire room) and 238, *Le Tombeau des Lutteurs* (full color plate, half page, showing red rose occupying entire room), both plates, 161.

Lines 17-20:   more than a little judgmental, toward unidentified acquaintances, in a matter that can concern the poet only as a personal anxiety. Cf. "KZ Oratorio," 64, 7 (also 66, 10); 81, 23 (also 87, 14 and the note on this latter passage). See also the note on "Love's Desert."

"Harbach 1944" (39-40; 21, 23)

A: *Trapeze and Parallel Bars* (later transferred to *On the Third Day*).
Without citing, Tüskés (104, 106, 111) writes that the poem first appeared in *Magyarok*.

Dedicatee: Gábor Thurzó (1912-1979), writer, translator, three-time winner of the Attila József Prize (in 1953, 1958, 1967), collaborator with JP on the mastheads of several Budapest literary magazines, among them *Élet, Ezüstkor, Vigilia* (see *KMÍK*; Tüskés 49-53, with photo, 50).

Title: As Czigány (15) points out, there are two places named Harbach, one near the Austrian-Czech border and one near Salzburg. The latter location is intended.

Comment: "Pilinszky-portré a televízióban" ("P. Portrait on Television"; interview with Gyula Maár), *Convv*. 238-41 (JP concludes interview by reading "Harbach 1944"); Fülöp 76-78; Kuklay 79-82; Pomogáts; Tüskés 82-83.

Stanza 1, genre picture: may be taken literally. Tüskés reports that JP met the unfortunates he depicts. See also the Introduction.

Lines 3-4:   invite comparison with poetry by Anthony Hecht. See the Introduction, and n. 36.

Lines 10, 17-20:   personification of nature.

Lines 21-24:   close observation, actual experience. Cf. "Fish in a Net," lines 11-12: "Our writhing wounds, / strangles our sibling."

Line 28 "troughs":   cf. "Paraphrase," line 13, and the note there.

"French Prisoner" (40-41; 25, 27)

A: *Válasz* (Reply) 7, no. 3 (March 1947): 233, as "Csak azt feledném" ("Could I But Forget That One"). *

The poem is translated in *Anthologie de la Poésie hongroise du XIIᵉ siècle a nos jours*, ed. Ladislas Gara (Paris: Éditions du Seuil, 1962) 416-17 ("Un P. G. Français," trans. Anne-Marie de Backer). On this anthology see also the notes on "Apocrypha" and "Afterword."

Comment: Fülöp 71-73; S. Radnóti 92-93; Tüskés 84: "It is in the UNRRA camp at Frankfurt that he sees the unfortunate man who had escaped from French captivity, and whom the American camp police soon returned." Tüskés (211) also adverts to two articles that JP wrote in 1960: "Nem vétkezünk többé" ("We Shall Transgress No More") and "Éhség" ("Hunger") (*Nadir* 1:75-77, 81-84). The same two essays will also help interpret "Frankfurt."

Lines 1, 38 "the Frenchman": this may be erroneous. Tüskés (84) is most probably right in mentioning "French captivity"; that is, it may well have been a French prisoner-of-war camp, which could make the prisoner in the poem a German. Cf. Backer's title "Un P. G. Français" (in Gara's anthology, cited above). An argument that a Frenchman detained by the French could be a deserter would not work, since a deserter would most probably be shot.

Lines 13-16, 25-28, juxtaposition of delight and torment: cf. "Frankfurt."

Line 32, autophagy: cf. the suggestion of cannibalism in "Paraphrase."

Lines 37-38: self-conscious report on the creative process.

"On a KZ Lager's Wall" (41-42; 29)

A: *Vigilia* 15, no. 12 (December 1950): 663, as "Ravensbrück (Egy halottra)" ("Ravensbrück [To One Dead]");

Kortárs (Contemporary) 1, no. 10 (October 1957): 207, as "Majdanek."*

Comment: Fülöp 79-82; S. Radnóti 92.

Stanza 1, insistent language, suggestion of irretrievability: cf. "From the Henchman's Diary," lines 1-4.

Line 5 "The land flees you": cf. "Harbach 1944," stanzas 5-8 (personified landscape).

Line 6, catalogue: cf. "Infernó" (*CP* 125), lines 1-2: "House. Dog. Car. / Lawn and receptions"; also "Enough," line 3, and "Two Portraits" (section "*Brontë*").

Line 10 "Did we blind you? You hold us with your eyes": Oedipus theme? See JP's article "Ödipusz ma" ("Oedipus Today") (*Nadir* 1:525-26). In JP's poetic vision, the eye is important from start to finish.

Line 12, motif of testimony: cf. "Without Witnesses," lines 9-12, where witnesses are introduced in the subjunctive.

"Ravensbrück Passion" (42; 31)

A: *Kortárs* 3, no. 6 (June 1959): 904.

Title: "Ravensbrück:" names yet another camp; cf. Harbach, Frankfurt, Auschwitz, Majdanek. Ravensbrück also receives glancing allusion in line 2 of "Harmadnapon" ("On the Third Day") (*CP* 42). "Passion": touches on Passion versus Holocaust, in whose equivalence JP strongly believed. Cf. "On the Third Day" and "Cattle Brand."

Line 2 "cube silence": cf. cube imagery in "KZ Oratorio," speech by Young Boy (64, 9-16; 83, 2-9).

Line 3 "projected picture": evocation of a newsreel, as well as of personal experience at the camp named? Newsreels were popular in postwar Budapest, and the camps were a subject frequently covered.

Line 6 "pores": cf. "Under a Portrait," line 8 "the pores' brutal veil of lace," and the note there.

Lines 7, 8 "gigantic" versus "minuscule": cf. "Apocrypha," 2.4-5 versus 8 (relative size predicated of trees, woods).

Stanza 3, execution by firing: cf. passage toward end of film script *Requiem* (*Nadir* 2:47).

"Frankfurt" (43-44; 33, 35, 37)

A: *Vigilia* 13, no. 7 (July 1948): 387-88.

Based on experience at UNRRA camp, Frankfurt am Main, 1945. Tüskés (88) tells us that JP was decently fed there, implying that he was thus not subject to the humiliations he depicts.

Comment: Fülöp 73-76; Tüskés 83-84.

Lines 6 "car," 18 "vehicle": not an automobile, but rather a truck in which camp personnel would take the trash out to the "landfill" (line 2).

Lines 14-15: cf. "KZ Oratorio," 66, 10-14; 87, 14-18 (Old Woman).

Line 24 "and were resurrected upside down": Is this a travesty of Saint Peter's martyrdom? It is not impossible, considering JP's religious and biblical system of reference.

Stanzas 4-5, "delight" and "rapture" conceits: cf. "French Prisoner."

Line 46 "the river": Hungarian *folyam* (rather than *folyó*) implies a major river, or the lower flow of such; it distinctly does not apply to the river Main (it seems more suitable, e.g., to the Rhine north of Cologne). JP's use of *folyam* may here be taken as a sign of the intense feeling expressed in such poems of wartime suffering as "Frankfurt" and "French Prisoner."

Stanzas 6-8, summer imagery: cf. the feeling in "Love's Desert."

Lines 59-60, conceit of "darkening paradise": cf. "dark heaven" in "Te győzz le" ("You Be the One to Defeat Me") (*CP* 9), closing line; and in "KZ Oratorio," 67, 29; 91, 9 (the young girl, M. R.).

Concluding line, *"Frankfurt—1945"*: an "Ecce Homo" gesture not dissimilar to the close of "Harbach 1944." As Ted Hughes so well puts it in his Introduction to JP's 1976 *Selected Poems*: "Whatever he met in those camps evidently opened the seventh seal for Pilinszky" (9).

"Fragment from the Golden Age" (44-45; 39)

A: *Vigilia* 14, no. 2 (February 1949): 97-98.

Dedicatee: "U. E.": most probably Ernő Urbán (1918-1974), journalist, populist writer, from 1953 on the editorial board of *Csillag*, to which JP contributed. With JP he shares Catholic background; like the poet, EU too served in the military (and deserted). Their paths could have crossed at the University. A prolific writer, EU was a recipient of the Kossuth Prize (in 1952, for journalism) and of the Attila József Prize (1971) (*MÉL; KMÍK*).

Comment: Kuklay 270-71 (quotes *Convv.* 240-41, at the end of which JP recites poem); S. Radnóti 86-87 (stresses the internal contradictoriness of the lexicon; calls attention to kinship of poem with "Elysium in November," especially on the count of sun imagery); Tandori, 1983, 363-65.

Line 11 "kennel": cf. "Apocrypha," 1.4 "the silence of the kennels"; on the importance of this image, see Tüskés 83. Cf. also "Love's Desert" and "Enough," and the notes there.

Lines 14, 16, repeated words: in the original, line 14 "dobog, dobog" (lit. "beats, beats") and 16 "szorít, szorít" ("squeezes, squeezes"). Cf., e.g., "A tenger" ("The Sea") (*CP* 70), line 12 and, immediately following, "Metropolitan Icons," section "*Museum.*" Line 7 repeats line 3, and there is threefold repetition of a word in line 10. Word repetition is a vehicle of strong feeling in JP's poetic practice.

Lines 23-24 "As at a gallows, so blinding it is, / and so sweet": cf. contrasting gallows images in "A Little Night Music," "From the Henchman's Diary," "The Henchman's Room," and "Gallows in Winter."

"Love's Desert" (46-47; 41)

A: *Csillag* (Star) 10, no. 7 (July 1956): 68.

Title: Given to title of the 1989 reprint of the Hughes-Csokits *Selected Poems* (main title: *The Desert of Love*).

Comment: JP's essay "Napfogyatkozás" ("Solar Eclipse") (*Nadir* 1:441); Csokits 1989; Nemes Nagy 1988; S. Radnóti 87-89; 88.

Line 1: cf. the opening of "Frankfurt," also stanzas 6-8.

Lines 2-3, personification imagery, as in "Harbach 1944"; also "emptying one's pockets": could this recall military frisking and impounding?

Lines 10-12, 16 birds and wings: cf. JP's statement on quality versus quantity in creativity, *Convv.* 22.

Line 21 "hope": cf. "Apocrypha," 2.23 "hope," namely, that the speaker will ever see his beloved. In "Love's Desert," the statement on "hope" is stronger—it constitutes an implicit denial that the poet and the woman he loves will ever be able to share their lives. The two poems are separated only by "Noon" and "Revelation 8:7."

On JP's own largely unsuccessful relations with women, see Tüskés: on Anna Márkus (125-28), on Jutta Schärer (233-37), on Sheryl Sutton (275-79), and on Ingrid Fichieux (282-85). All of these relations, including JP's two marriages (to Márkus and to Fichieux), became lasting platonic friendships.

Tüskés's long paragraph on Márkus includes an allusion to "Love's Desert" (127).

"Noon" (47; 43)

A: *Új Ember* (New Man), 15-20 August 1960.

Comment: S. Radnóti 87-88.

Lines 3-12, personifying language: cf. sun and roof imagery in "Fragment from the Golden Age."

Line 23 "outline" (Hungar. *rajz*, lit. "drawing"): cf. "Without Witnesses," line 1.

Line 24 "my gaunt earthly presence": cf. "Poetic Presence," JP's interview with Mátyás Domokos (*Convv.* 91-110).

"Revelation 8:7" (48; 45)

A: *On the Third Day.*

Comment: Kuklay 78 (explains reason for lack of capitalization and punctuation throughout poem, the latter being intended as a direct continuation of biblical text); S. Radnóti 111.

Title: Revelation 8:7 (King James Version): "The first angel sounded, and there followed hail and fire mingled with blood, and they were cast upon the earth: and the third part of trees was burnt up, and all green grass was burnt up."

Some of the apocalyptic imagery in this poem: cf. that in the opening lines of "Apocrypha."

Lines 11-12, suggestion of God's own immanence and "limitation": cf. "Every Breath," stanza 2.

"Apocrypha" (48-50; 47, 49, 51, 53)

A: *Csillag* 10, no. 7 (July 1956): 67.

Comment: *Convv.* 10-16; Fülöp 88-102; Németh G.; S. Radnóti 89, 91-92, 100, 110-11; Tandori, 1983, 366-68.

Translated, in Gara's French-language anthology (see note on "French Prisoner"), by Pierre Emmanuel (417-19). The date line ("juin 1956") cites the year of first appearance. The poem was written in 1954 (*Convv.* 14).

1.1-8: These lines allude to the language of Revelation.

1.4 "the silence of the kennels": see Tüskés 83.

1.30 "prison uniform": Is there the hint of a contradiction here with JP's statement that he was never an inmate at any of the camps (*Convv.* 16)?

2.1-2, evocation of infancy and childhood: it is a time important for JP, one he gladly treats in verse or discusses in prose. See "Sketch"; *Convv.* 128-29; *Nadir* 2:232 (index entries "child," "childlike").

2.11: refers to the poet's return from the war. Cf. the title of JP's interview with Rezső Forgács (*Convv.* 111-22).

2.12: alludes to the parable of the Prodigal Son (Luke 15:11-32). Cf. "Looking for the Prodigal Son," and the note there.

2.19-26, theme of love: see S. Radnóti 97-99 (quotes passage, 98). On its problematic nature, see the note on "Love's Desert."

2.23 "hope": cf. "Love's Desert," line 21.

2.26 "Like a wild beast, I am scared, alert": cf. 1.8 "as a watchful wild animal, so tranquil." Cf. also "Noon," line 6 "its wild-animal attentiveness ..."

2.33 "I don't understand human speech": cf. Hölderlin, "Da ich ein Knabe war," line 27 "Der Menschen Worte verstand ich nie" (Hanser 1:167-68; 168). If the carry-over is real, it suggests that JP read the poem in German, since by 1954 he could have seen the translation by György Rónay only in a magazine, if at all. JP's source most probably was: *Friedrich Hölderlins Sämtliche Werke,* ed. [after the Insel edition of Franz Zinkernagel] Friedrich Michael (Leipzig: Insel, n.d. [1922], with printings up to the early 1940s) (Sarkowski 740). Rónay's translation of "Da ich ein Knabe war" will be found in: *Friedrich Hölderlin Versei* (Poems of F. H.), ed. György Rónay, Lyra Mundi series (Budapest: Európa, 1980) 38-39. On JP's affinity with the German poet, see also the notes on "Under a Winter Sky," "Celebration of Nadir," and "Hölderlin."

2.35 "the Word": not capitalized in the original, but Scripture is clearly one level of meaning.

3.1, 9-10, images: cf. "Afterword," lines 1-4 (comment, S. Radnóti 120), and the note there.

"Four-Liner" (51; 55)
A: *Csillag* 10, no. 7 (July 1956): 69.
Comment: Kuklay 123-28; Nemes Nagy, 1988; Tamás; Tüskés 128-34.
Kuklay alights in part on JP's difficulties with women and marriage (cites JP's statement that line 4 has to do with his coming divorce), but touches also on the Christ in Gethsemane theme. Tüskés concentrates on the parallels between Jesus' Passion and JP's personal martyrdom, but questions the value of biographical data for an understanding of line 4. Like Tüskés, Tamás undertakes a careful structural analysis, pointing out the role of extraordinary compression of language in the poem.

"Under a Portrait" (51; 57)
A: *Vigilia* 22 (1957): 735.
Line 1 "the graphite of dusk": a powerful image or metaphor by which JP treats the end or beginning of day; cf. "Love's Desert," line 4 "the catatonic twilight"; "Apocrypha," 1.26 "the infrared of an angry sky."
Lines 3 "sea," 9 "waves": cf. "Every Breath," lines 3-4.
Lines 5-8, image of the poet's face: without citing, Tüskés (179) reports: "it is from György Rónay's article we know that in the lines from 'Under a Portrait' [quotes stanza 2] it is Alyosha Karamazov's portrait that [JP] draws with deep expertise" (also Tüskés 147). See Rónay, 1971, 331-33; also Fyodor Dostoyevsky, *The Brothers Karamazov*, trans. David McDuff (London, New York: Penguin, 1993), pt. 3, bk. 7, chap. 1 (375-88; 377). Cited as Penguin and page. More on Alyosha Karamazov in "Elysium in November."
Line 10 "worm": see the notes on "To Two Lovers" and "Definition."

"Imperfect Tense" (52; 59)

A: *Vigilia* 22 (1957): 735.

Dedicatee: The appearance of the poem in book form predates the inscription to Ted Hughes (the English poet, b. 1930) by a decade. JP and TH first met in London, at Poetry International, in 1969 (Tüskés 205-06). Despite the language barrier, there was immediate rapport between the two poets, partly on account of their shared enthusiasm for Simone Weil (Tüskés 206). On TH, see also JP's second interview with László Cs. Szabó, "Versünk a világban" ("Our Poem in the World") (*Convv.* 44-70; 49-51).

Comment: Rónay, 1971, 328-31; Tandori, 1983, 365-66 (with comment on title); Tüskés 170-71.

Lines 3-4 "a single, enormous blow− / the moon": cf. "KZ Oratorio," Old Woman: "A single, enormous blow!" (63, 22; 81, 8, also 68, 26; 93, 10).

Lines 12, 13, 15 "You are combing your hair," especially in lines 14, 15 "mirror": is the person addressed female? Does it matter, as it does in "Jewel"? See the note on this poem below.

Lines 14, 15 "in a mirror," "in your mirror," surreal effect. The passage can be construed as: "inside the world of said mirror only, and not at the same time within the reality that the mirror is supposed to be mirroring." In that case "mirror," likened in line 16 to "a glass coffin," would also resemble "monstrance" and "diamond-empty museum," as in "Metropolitan Icons." See also "Perpetuum mobile" and note.

"Elysium in November" (53; 61)

A: *Új Ember*, 8 February 1959.

Comment: *Nadir* 2:226 (index entries for Dostoyevsky); S. Radnóti 87-88; Tüskés 179.

Date line under poem: A rare occurrence in JP's work; cf. "A Little Night Music." Significant for the poem is the place designation "*Szigliget*," the site of a famous sanatorium.

Lines 8-11, comparison with Alyosha Karamazov: cf. the four chapters of bk. 7 of the novel (Penguin 375-418).

Line 15 "to gleam": cf. "Afterword," line 32 "Gleam−in vain!" More on "gleaming" in "Stavrogin Returns."

Line 17 "like the blessed": this suggestion of an invented, one-person Paradiso is one of JP's most appealing genre pictures. See the Introduction.

from *Metropolitan Icons* (1970)

"Afterword" (57-58; 65, 67)

A: *Új Írás* (New Writing) 2, no. 9 (September 1962): 961.

Dedicatee: Pierre Emmanuel (1916-1984), poet, translator, seminal essayist. JP became acquainted with PE in Paris, in the summer of 1963. On the good fellowship between the two poets, see *Nadir* 1:195, 209, 211, 321-23. In *Convv.* (64), JP confesses that the part of PE's oeuvre and thought that draws him most are the essays. He may be alluding to: Pierre Emmanuel, *Le Monde est intérieur: Essais* (Paris: Éditions du Seuil, 1967), especially to the essays with religious concerns in the third and closing part, "Perspective" (231-313). It is also of some interest to note that PE visited Budapest in November of 1964; see Rónay, *Diaries*, 2:764-65.

Title: The poem is best understood as a poetic "Afterword" to Ladislas Gara's French-language anthology of Hungarian poetry (1962), for which PE translated "Apocrypha." The presumable publication date of Gara's volume predates 1 September (see the imprint and *dépôt légal* notice, p. 503); JP appears to have written the poem almost immediately upon receipt of his copy, as a gesture of thanks to PE.

Comment: *Convv.* 222-26; S. Radnóti 117-18 (rhythm); Tandori, 1983, 368-69. The observations on the significance of the title and the reason for resemblances in language between "Afterword" and "Apocrypha" are mine.

Lines 1-4 "Do you still remember?": Your translating activity and its problems, especially in section 3 of the poem you were working on. The phrases and sentences "on the faces," "the empty ditch," "it's trickling down," and "I'm standing in the sun" all occur in "Apocrypha," in 3.8 (in PE: 3.7), 3.10, 3.10, and 3.1, respectively. S. Radnóti (120), who notes this amazing set

216

of resemblances, does not note the reason for them.

Stanzas 2-6: they depict a visit with PE in Paris, imagined a good nine months prior to its actually taking place.

Line 12, metaphor: comparison of someone's back with a tombstone: cf. "Sírkövemre" ("On My Gravestone") (*CP* 115), lines 4-5: "wipe from God's back, wipe off / my shameful memory."

Line 19 "my face, this stone": for another face-stone metaphor, see "Apocrypha," 3.5-8 (there, the whole being is of stone).

Lines 30-32, motif of gleaming: see S. Radnóti 121. See also Rónay, *Diaries*, 2:416, on JP's "gleaming fragments."

Lines 37-38, theme of love and friendship: cf. S. Radnóti 98.

On PE as a translator of JP's work, Tüskés (193) quotes from a presumable 1963 diary entry by JP to the effect that PE has invited him, "so that we can discuss in peace and quiet the translation problems of my oratorio." The visit took place in Paris sometime between 1963 and 1967. PE did evidently prepare a translation of "KZ Oratorio" (see Csokits, 1992, 19, 26, 27, and Czigány 12), but it came too late for inclusion in Gara's anthology, and may well have remained in manuscript.

With PE, JP also shares an interest in Hölderlin; see the former's *Le Poète Fou* (1944); in English translation: Pierre Emmanuel, *The Mad Poet*, trans. Elliott Coleman, Contemporary Poetry Library Series, 11 (Baltimore: Contemporary Poetry, 1956).

"Introit" (58; 69)

A: *Vigilia* 26 (1961): 712.

Comment: Kuklay (75-77) quotes Revelation 4:9-5:10, in the Hungarian Catholic version of the Bible, thus identifying the poem's scriptural source.

Title: Alludes to the opening movement of the requiem mass; here, it is a proper opener for a work that immediately precedes "KZ Oratorio." "*Introit*" is also the title of the cycle in which both poems occur. This ordering carefully follows the printing in *Metropolitan Icons*, and reflects JP's intentions.

"KZ Oratorio" (59-69; 71-95)

A: *Új Írás* 2, no. 12 (December 1962): 1365-72, as "Sötét mennyország" ("Dark Heaven").

The work was first performed at Kecskemét, at the József Katona Gimnázium, in the spring of 1963, in the presence of the poet (see Tüskés 175, with photo). *Title, genre*: Cf. Sándor Sík, *Advent: Oratorium szavalókórusra* (Advent: Oratorio for Recitation Chorus), SzFMK, Színpad-Könyvtár (Stage Library), 3 (Szeged: Szegedi Fiatalok Művészeti Kollégiuma [Szeged Youth Arts College], 1935).

Language, concerns: Images and turns of phrase are often borrowed from earlier poetry (e.g., "A single, enormous blow!" [63, 22; 81, 8]; cf. "Imperfect Tense," lines 3-4, and note). In form and style, "KZ Oratorio" is close to the surrealism and minimalism of the four plays in *Dénouement*, especially to *Tableaux Vivants*, but it is very distant in style from *Requiem*, the one major work most closely related to "KZ Oratorio" in theme.

Comment: *Convv.* 16-21; Domonkos and Valaczka; Fülöp 184-86; Kuklay 138-39, 158-59; Tüskés 172-73.

59, 22, 24; 71, 22, 24, on "shaking nails": for a view that these have nothing to do with the nails of the cross, see Domonkos and Valaczka 535; on "light bulbs" (60, 22; 73, 22), see 537.

60, 16 through 62, 10; 73, 16 through 77, 20 "It was night when we left the city" through "and gave off light, like a monstrance": this is a report on the train trip of the three to the camp, and on their gassing, answering Young Boy's question "We're dead, aren't we?" (62, 31; 79, 14) in the affirmative. "KZ Oratorio" is a play (or: dialogue) of the dead. Cf. Jean-Paul Sartre's short novel *Les Jeux Sont Faits* (1947). JP read Sartre; see Tüskés 177.

61, 22 (also: 63, 18 and 68, 22); 77, 2 (also: 81, 4 and 93, 6) "turnkey peasants": in the original, *porkolábparasztok*. Hungarian *porkoláb*, "jailer," "turnkey," is related etymologically to German *Burggraf*, "burgrave," "feudal lord"; peasants in the service of one such were often employed as jailkeepers. Here, "turnkey peasants" may be taken to connote men and women of the peasantry who made their services available to the SS. For help with the linguistic aspects of this note I am indebted to Professor Robert Austerlitz, Columbia University.

62, 12-29; 77, 22 through 79, 12, tale of the pure-hearted wolf: see Kuklay

158-59 (under "Fabula"); cf. also "For Jutta," section "*January*," lines 2-5, and the note on this passage.

64, 9-16; 83, 2-9, Young Boy on "seven cubes": boxcars. Other levels of interpretation: rooms in a dream; realms of consciousness. For other cube conceits in JP's work, see "cube silence" ("Ravensbrück Passion"); and "prickling hot cube" ("Parable") (*CP* 91).

64, 18 through 65, 4; 83, 11 through 85, 3: developed love motif. Coming on us unawares, 64, 22; 83, 15 "elveszíthetem" ("I may [or: could] lose him") introduces the love sequence. Although the Hungarian form *elveszíthetem* is indeterminate as to gender, and does also mean "I could lose it," only the masculine makes sense in context. This is clear also from 65, 2 "Törd rá az ajtót!" (83, 26 "Break down his door!"); the girl and old woman are talking about a man, and not about an abstract "it."

66, 10; 87, 14 "don't judge me!": cf. "Judge not, that ye be not judged" (Matthew 7:1); also JP's essay "Ne ítéljetek!" ("Do Not Judge!") (*Nadir* 1:413-14; dated 5 September 1971). (See also Kuklay 138-39.) JP's piece discusses the *clochards* of Paris—the homeless of his day—very much in the spirit of Matthew and the passage in "KZ Oratorio." On "being judgmental," see *Nadir* 2:233 (index).

66, 11-14; 87, 15-18: cf. "French Prisoner" and "Frankfurt," and the notes there.

66, 24-25; 87, 28-89, 1, mirror imagery: cf. "Afterword," stanza 5; also "Imperfect Tense."

67, 29; 91, 9 "My dark heaven": the wording of the original title of "KZ Oratorio"; cf. also the last line of the first poem in *CP*, "Te gyözz le" ("You Be the One to Defeat Me") (9). On this, see also the Introduction.

69, 16-20; 95, 6-10, Young Boy's aria: see Tüskés 34. Is there something of a suggestion here of a Bach cantata, even of the *Christmas Oratorio*? The boy's aria is an image of inner birth, of the awakening of consciousness. On JP's affinity with J. S. Bach, see *Nadir* 2:225 (index), also *Convv.* 156-57, 183.

On Simone Weil's putative influence on "KZ Oratorio," dating from a time when JP was not yet acquainted with her writings, see *Convv.* 52. JP thoroughly approved of the insight of the Yugoslav critic who made the observation.

"Metropolitan Icons" (70-71; 97, 99)

A: *Kortárs* 7, no. 2 (February 1963): 199.

Title: Alludes indirectly to JP's confessed affinity with icon painting, rather than with the more dynamic movements in painting since the trecento (*Convv.* 14). Chosen as the title of the present selection.

    Comment: S. Radnóti 100-03 (102: quotes section "*Museum*," stanzas 1-3).

    Section "*Three A.M.*," both lines, Magrittean effect: cf. René Magritte, *The Idol* (1965), oil on canvas, showing a bird of stone in flight over a beach strewn with rocks, as in: Pere Gimferrer, *Magritte* (New York: Rizzoli, 1987), no. 136 (color reproduction over an unpaginated opening). Identified at top left; also to rear of volume (128). On Magritte, see also the notes on "To Two Lovers" and "The Henchman's Room," and the Introduction.

    Section "*Museum*," stanzas 1-3, word repetitions: see the note on "Fragment from the Golden Age."

    "*Museum*," line 12: the Garden of Gethsemane is undoubtedly meant.

    "*Museum*," lines 13-14: this suggestive language recurs in JP's mature poetry; cf. only "Spaces." See also the Introduction.

    Location: Strong feeling of Budapest, although by February 1963 he could also be recalling Rome. For a similar problem, see the note on "Admonition."

"Van Gogh" (71; 101)

A: *Új Írás* 3, no. 12 (December 1963): 1490.

Title: On Vincent Van Gogh and JP's affinity with his art, see *Convv.* 51, 173; *Nadir* 2:230 (index); Tüskés 179 (with reproductions of a self-portrait of the artist, 178, and of Van Gogh's painting of his shoes, 180). See also JP's essay "Versailles, Chartres, Paris" (*Nadir* 1:211-13; 212). More on JP's experience of Van Gogh in the note on "Van Gogh's Prayer."

    2.5 "iron ball": cf. "Game," "Miss I. B.," and the notes on these poems.

    3.1 "'Lamb of the world'": cf. "Introit" and "The Henchman's Room."

    3.2 "'the present tense'": intense attention to language and grammar; cf. "Imperfect Tense" and "Infinitive," and the notes there.

"A Little Night Music" (72; 103)

A: *Piarista Öregdiák* (Piarist Alumnus) 1966: 31, as "Egy kis éjizene" (rather than: "Kis éjizene," the title here). Either version translates into English as above.

Allusion in title: On Mozart, see *Nadir* 2:228 (index); Kuklay 168-70; Tüskés 191-93 (quoting *Nadir* 1:212-13, a portion of the "Versailles, Chartres, Paris" article, quoted also in Kuklay 169). The article, for *Új Ember*, dates from 25 August 1963, after JP's return from France.

Opening and closing lines of poem, "O gallows-fragrance!": cf. "The Henchman's Room," line 5 "the fragrance of the gallows," the passages in both poems near images of flowers (there: geraniums, line 1). The suggestion that Mozart was "executed" is strong, and establishes a parallel with other artists who died young (Radnóti, József) and, not last, with Jesus.

Section *"Dialogue"*: cf. "Two Portraits," section *"Brontë,"* lines 2, 9-10.

Section *"Midnight,"* line 5 "billiard balls": cf. "Game" and "Miss I. B.," and the notes on both.

Section *"Mozart"*: cf. *Nadir* 1:212-13, the experience of the visit as recounted there.

"Mozart," line 5, inscription (actually, a wall plaque): cf. *Nadir* 1:213, there in the wording: "Mozart habita en cette maison en 1763" (with a translation into Hungarian in the next line).

"White Pietà" (72; 105)

A: *Metropolitan Icons* 141.

Title: It may allude to JP's experience of Michelangelo's statue *Pietà* in Saint Peter's Basilica in Rome. He first saw it on his early trip to Italy, in late autumn of 1947 (see Tüskés 106-09, with photo showing JP and friends in front of Saint Peter's, 108). On Michelangelo, see JP's review "Michelangelo Buonarotti versei" ("The Poems of M. B.") (*Nail & Oil* 21; not in *Nadir*): "From the *David* to the rough-hewn, wonderful *Pietà*—this precisely is the road of the poet Michelangelo as well." The review dates from 10 January 1960.

Lines 2-3 make it intrinsically probable that the poem does record JP's experience of Michelangelo's statue.

Line 4 "laterna magica": A film projector? JP has an article titled "Laterna mágika" ("Magic Lantern"), dated 4 February 1962 (see *Nail & Oil*, bibliography of JP's articles, 478), but the text is not to be found in either collection of the prose.

"Passion" (73; 107)

A: *Metropolitan Icons* 145.

Comment: Kuklay 130, who connects the poem with Christ's Passion. That is one implication, but the matter goes beyond it, into modern history.

Line 2 "geranium smell": cf. "The Henchman's Room," and the note there.

Line 3 "glass": one of JP's favorite images; cf., e.g., "Imperfect Tense," "Perpetuum mobile."

Line 4 "the butcher's assistants wash up": as Pilate washed his hands of the case of Jesus (Kuklay), so do the numerous "butcher's assistants," that is, petty bourgeoisie who helped run the camps, once again feign innocence and pretend they knew little or nothing of what they helped make possible. For a list of the "assistants," by civilian occupations, see William Styron, *Sophie's Choice* (New York: Bantam, 1980) 182-83.

Line 5: see the Introduction. The poem is one of JP's most powerful indictments.

"From the Henchman's Diary" (74; 109)

A: *Metropolitan Icons* 147.

Dedicatee: Thomas [*sic*; Tomas] Tranströmer (b. 1931), distinguished Swedish poet and translator. TT's volume *Stigar* (Paths) (1973) contains his translations of poems by Robert Bly, and (with Géza Thinsz) by JP, with whose work TT "feels affinity" (*CDMEL*). TT and JP met in Stockholm, with the help of GTh, at the beginning of the 1970s. Géza Thinsz (b. 1934) is a noted Hungarian-Swedish writer, poet, and translator (*KMÍK*).

Comment: Kuklay 131.

Lines 1-4, insistent language: cf. "On a KZ Lager's Wall," stanza 1.

Line 5 "the clocks": images such as clock and metronome are a sign in JP's poetry that he is not concerned with the measurement of earthly time. Cf. "Metronome," lines 1-2.

Lines 8-9, see Kuklay's engaging interpretation: the henchman has entered eternity as soon as he has put the nails (diamonds) into the cross (crown).

"Holy Thief" (74; 111)

A: *Metropolitan Icons* 149.

Dedicatee: Mari Törőcsik (b. 1935), prize-winning stage and film actress, friend of JP. From the end of the 1950s to JP's death, a close platonic friendship united them. Especially during the 1970s and up to the last years, JP would be a frequent guest of Törőcsik and of her husband, the film director Gyula Maár, at their residence in Velem, in western Hungary. JP was also godfather to their daughter (information kindly provided by Dr. Péter Kovács in a letter). More on MT in *Nadir* 1:351, 429. On Gyula Maár, see the note on "Two Portraits."

Comment: Kuklay 97-101. The comparison with T. S. Eliot, "Burnt Norton" (98), is also applicable to imagery in "Crater."

Line 1 "By then": by the time Jesus spoke to him (see the note on lines 11-12).

Line 1 "him": the thief crucified to the right of Jesus, the one who repented and won grace. Kuklay (97) quotes Luke 23:32-43, discusses "the right-hand thief" (Hungarian *jobbik* also means "better"), and quotes from JP's essay "A jobbik lator" ("The Thief to His Right") (*Nadir* 1:325-26), along with a portion of Eliot's "Burnt Norton." JP's article dates from 26 March 1967 ("1976" [Kuklay 101] is erroneous).

Lines 2, 3 "beyond"; also negatives, lines 7 "neither" and 9 "nor": all point to the situs of the right-hand thief throughout the poem.

Lines 11-12 "friend, / friendship forever": "And he said unto Jesus, Lord, remember me when thou comest into thy kingdom. And Jesus said unto him, Verily I say unto thee, To day shalt thou be with me in paradise" (Luke 23:42-43). This is accomplished before line 1 of "Holy Thief" opens.

from *Splinters* (1972)

Title of collection: "splinters, that is, from the cross" (Hughes 9).

"As I Began" (87; 115)

A: *Splinters* 7.

Comment: S. Radnóti 80-81, 120-21.

The poem opens *Splinters*; there, it is in a precarious and even ironically exposed position. Totally at variance with what it seems to be saying, it is, in fact, the debut of a new poet, the author of the last three books.

Lines 1-2: S. Radnóti (120-21, quoting lines 1-2 on 120) defends and explains the paradoxical nature of the poetic opener.

Lines 3-5, simile: a reduced image of the soldier and captive returning to his city ("Apocrypha," section 2).

Line 4 "keeps on being silent": there is a deceptive link here with the poet's doubts concerning the word, as expressed in "Apocrypha." In the past, he certainly kept silent for various reasons, but the statement here is again self-contradictory. It is with this poem that JP breaks his two spells of silence (1949-1956 and 1959-1970), and breaks out into unprecedented poetic productivity. "As I Began" poses, as it well should, the in part unresolvable question of truth versus fiction in poetic self-portraiture.

"For Jutta" (87-88; 117)

A: *Splinters* 8.

Dedicatee in title: Jutta Schärer (Csokits 1992: Scherrer), of East German birth; church historian, polyglot intellectual, Slavist by avocation; settles in Paris, where JP becomes acquainted with her; teaches at Sorbonne (Tüskés 234; photo, 233). On JS's and JP's long-lasting friendship, in Paris, see Csokits 1992, and Czigány.

Comment: Kuklay (see individual sections below); S. Radnóti 84-85.

Section *"Letter"*: Kuklay (274-75; 275) quotes from JP's essay "Forgiveness and Forgetting" (*Nadir* 1:455-56).

Section "*January*," lines 2-5: cf. M. R.'s, the young girl's, tale of the pure-hearted wolf in "KZ Oratorio" (62, 12-29; 77, 22 through 79, 12). For juxtaposition of wolves and the Mass, cf. "The Way Only" (106-07; 149).

Section "*Fragment from a Diary*": A close prose version of all nine lines of this section will be found in JP's article "Egy lírikus naplójából" ("From a Lyrist's Diary"), *Nadir* 1:397-98; 398 (closing paragraph). The essay, one of numerous pieces bearing this title, dates from 17 January 1971; the poem "For Jutta" was, very possibly, written up to a year later.

"*Fragment from a Diary*," lines 4-6, Simone Weil quotation: Kuklay (90) quotes, in the translation by Ferenc Szabó, the following passage from Weil's essay "L'Amour de Dieu et le malheur" ("The Love of God and Affliction"):

> The man whose soul remains oriented towards God while a nail is driven through it finds himself nailed to the very centre of the universe; the true centre, which is not in the middle, which is not in space and time, which is God. In a dimension which is not spatial and which is not time, a totally other dimension, the nail has pierced through the whole of creation, through the dense screen which separates the soul from God.
>
> In this marvellous dimension, without leaving the time and place to which the body is bound, the soul can traverse the whole of space and time and come into the actual presence of God.
>
> It is at the point of intersection between creation and Creator. This point is the point of intersection of the two branches of the Cross.

(from *The Simone Weil Reader*, ed. George A. Panichas [New York: David McKay, 1977] 439-68; 452 [last three paragraphs]). JP read the essay in French; it is not yet included in Weil's *Œuvres Complètes* (in progress with Gallimard). For bibliographic information on the essay, see Panichas 511.

There is no questioning of the importance of SW for JP. On her, see also the poem "S. W.-hez" ("To S[imone] W[eil]") (*CP* 122); *Nadir* 2:230 (index); and Tüskés 195-98 (with portrait, 194). Weil lived from 1909 to 1943; but although her life was of Mozartean brevity, she is held to be one of the century's most important philosophers.

"Celebration of Nadir" (90; 119)

A: *Splinters* 14.

Title: Kuklay (248-49) juxtaposes the poem with an excerpt from JP's article "J. S. Bach" (*Nadir* 1:298-99; dates from 13 March 1966): "[Bach's] art is the 'celebration of nadir'" (299). This is a reinterpretation of the concept, inverting the value of "depth-point" that seems to be assayed in the poem.

The title of this poem is that given to the two-volume edition of JP's journalistic and other prose, cited throughout this selection as *Nadir*.

Other comment: S. Radnóti 99.

Line 1 "the bloodstained warmth of the barns" (*ólak* also connotes "kennels"): cf. "Apocrypha," 1.4, and the note there.

Line 2 "who dare read?": autobiographical. See *Convv.* 113, 232, for JP's account of how, out west in 1944, he had taken along many books, only to throw them one by one out of the railroad car because they were "anachronistic," "not valid" (232; see also Tüskés 80, 82). (In that "not valid" one overhears today's "not relevant.") With line 2 "who dare read?" we also overhear "Introit," line 1 "Who will open the closed book?" It is the answer to this that inverts the value of "nadir."

Line 4 "splinter-meadow": the locus of Christ's Passion—and of ours. A future concordance of JP's poetic lexicon will find a number of occurrences of *splinter* in his 1972 collection.

Lines 11-15, human presences at line 10 "that nadir": cf. "The Seventh Circle of Hell"; also "Spaces." Much like Plato, JP urges that aspects of what we view as reality are but phenomena of a doomed world, not higher reality at all (see, e.g., *Convv.* 173).

Lines 19-20 "the sea / like a handful of water": the passage carries two references: first, Beethoven's calling Bach a "sea." This comes from an account of a visit paid Beethoven by Karl Gottfried (Hamburger: Gottlieb) Freudenberg, a young organist, in July of 1825, according to whom Beethoven said: "Not Bach (brook) but Meer (sea) should be his name, ..."; see Michael Hamburger (ed.), *Beethoven: Letters, Journals, Conversations* (Garden City, NY: Doubleday, Anchor Books, 1960) 239-40; 239; also *Thayer's Life of Beethoven*, ed. Elliot Forbes, 2 vols. (Princeton: Princeton UP, 1964), 2:955-56; 956. Second, JP's passage evokes the motto to Hölderlin's novel *Hyperion*, *oder Der Eremit in Griechenland*; the line, from the epitaph of Saint Ignatius of Loyola, reads: "Non coerceri maximo, contineri minimo, divinum est" ("Not to be constrained by the greatest, to be contained in the smallest, is divine") (Hanser 1:610). There can be no question that by 1972 JP knew *Hyperion* in the translation by Ede Szabó (Budapest: Európa, 1958), besides familiarity with the original. Cf. the notes on "Apocrypha," section 2, and "Hölderlin."

"The Henchman's Room" (91; 121)

A: *Splinters* 16.

Line 1: this juxtaposition is not new, nor are the sensations new individually. Cf. "A Little Night Music," "Passion," "Experience."

Lines 3-4, a distinctly Magrittean touch. See René Magritte, *La Condition Humaine*, 1933, oil on canvas, showing a window with an easel in front of it, with trompe l'oeil effect, reproduced in color in: Jacques Meuris, *Magritte* (n.p. [Paris]: Nouvelles Éditions Françaises, 1988) 144 (fig. 215).

Line 5 "the fragrance of the gallows": cf. the opening and closing lines of "A Little Night Music."

Line 6 "the lamb": cf. "Introit"; "Four-Liner" (by implication).

"Crime and Punishment" (93; 123)

A: *Splinters* 23, as yet without the dedication.

Dedicatee: Sheryl Sutton (b. 1950), African-American actress. JP became acquainted with her in Paris, probably in 1971, after having attended a performance of Robert Wilson's play *Le Régard du Sourd* (*Deafman Glance*), in which Sutton played a major role. A close friendship developed between JP and SS; see the imaginative reconstruction of the days of their friendship in JP's major prose work of 1977, *Beszélgetések Sheryl Suttonnal: Egy párbeszéd regénye* (trans. as *Conversations with Sheryl Sutton: The Novel of a Dialogue*). For citations of the complete text, in the original as well as in the published English translation, see the Bibliography.

Title: Although allusive, it has to do not with the novel by Dostoyevsky,

227

but with events as depicted in Robert Wilson's play (fatal stabbings). See Stefan Brecht, *The Original Theatre of the City of New York: From the Mid-60s to the Mid-70s, Book 1: The Theatre of Visions: Robert Wilson* (Frankfurt am Main: Suhrkamp, 1978) 54-140 (*"Deafman Glance"*); also Laurence Shyer, *Robert Wilson and His Collaborators* (New York: Theatre Communications Group, 1989) 4-15 ("Sheryl Sutton"), 253-67 ("Bob Wilson in France ..."), 288-317 ("Chronology and Works"). From the last-named (294) we learn that the Paris performances of *Deafman Glance* took place between 14-30 May and 11 June-3 July 1971. "While Wilson's talents had not gone unrecognized in New York it was in France that his reputation and fortunes were made. The appearance of *Deafman Glance* ... in Paris in May of 1971 created a sensation, ..." (253). It also won the "Prix de la Critique Française for best foreign play" (294).

Comment: JP's article "Új színház született" ("A New Theater Is Born") (*Nadir* 1:409-10; dated 8 August 1971); *Conversations with Sheryl Sutton* (*Nadir* 2:139-41), reprints translation of "Crime and Punishment" by Ted Hughes, with erroneous spelling in title, "PUNISHEMENT" (140; quietly corrected in Kuklay 291). "Sheryl found the poem dedicated to her beautiful, though a little overexposed" (*Nadir* 2:140; from chap. 6 of the dialogue-novel, as also cited in Kuklay 287-95; 290-91).

Line 8 "It's still summer": the "summer" of youth, the life of the deafmute young boy may well be meant by JP. For independent and yet related interpretive comment, see the Introduction.

Line 9 "scepter": again with reference to visual elements in Wilson's play, the knife with which the woman (Sheryl Sutton) is to stab the boy.

See also the poems "Hommage à Sheryl Sutton I" and "Hommage à Sheryl Sutton II" (*CP* 138, 138-39) and "Kőfal és ünnepély" ("Stone Wall and Celebration") (*CP* 92), the last-named with the dedicatory inscription "*Hommage à Robert Wilson.*" On RW, see also *Nadir* 1:409-13 and 2:133-89.

"Perpetuum mobile" (93; 125)

A: *Splinters* 24.

Title: The image is that of a paternoster elevator, common enough in Budapest, especially in banks and other public buildings.

Line 1, the World Bank: while its headquarters are in Washington, D. C., each country has a Field Office, and JP may have encountered one of these on his travels, possibly on his way from Paris to London between 1969 and 1971. See especially the article "Belgiumi képeslap" ("Postcard from Belgium") (*Nadir* 1:336-39). Nor is Holland excluded as a possibility; see the note on "Metronome."

Lines 3-7, similes: cf. what Blaise Cendrars does with the Eiffel Tower, in his "Tour" ("Tower") (August 1913), in *Dix-neuf Poèmes Élastiques* (1919); see *Selected Writings of Blaise Cendrars*, ed. Walter Albert (New York: New Directions, 1966) 140-45; also Blaise Cendrars, *Complete Poems*, trans. Ron Padgett, Introduction by Jay Bochner (Berkeley, Los Angeles: U of California P, 1992) 55-57. While JP must have been as aware of Cendrars as he was of Apollinaire (*Nadir* 1:184), he does not to my knowledge respond to the former.

Line 7: cf. JP's essay "A fáradtságról" ("On Being Tired") (*Nadir* 1:453).

"Metronome" (93; 127)

A: *Splinters* 25.

Comment: Kuklay 177-78; S. Radnóti 122-23 (123: quotes lines 7-8).

Lines 1-2: cf. JP on the element of time: "in poems you can do everything, but not time, really; that's an apparent time, it's like a Beethoven sonata; it lasts twenty minutes; that's an artificial time, a pseudo-time, not the time of the work" (from the radio interview with János Szilágyi, "Kettesben" ["In a Twosome"], *Convv.* 162-78; 167-68). The interview dates from 11 December 1978.

Line 4 "drawbridge": could allude either to Holland or to the painting by Van Gogh. This may help strengthen the supposition that JP did travel in Holland and did visit the local headquarters of the World Bank there (see above, note on "Perpetuum mobile").

Line 5: cf. "Gallows in Winter," but three poems following.

Lines 7-8: Kuklay concentrates on the larger religious import of the poem, and juxtaposes "Metronome" with JP's essay "A Genezis margójára" ("On the Margin of Genesis") (published in *Új Ember*, 23 January 1966; not in *Nadir*).

By "Genesis" JP means both the event and the First Book of Moses.

"Admonition" (94; 129)

A: *Békés megyei Népújság* (B. County People's News), 3 October 1971.

Comment: S. Radnóti 83.

Title: Admonition—to himself as a journalist, and as a "journalist" in poetry.

Lines 5, 6-9: Take notes on eternity, not on the passing moment. Cf. the preference, expressed in his essay "A 'teremtő képzelet' sorsa korunkban" ("The Fate of 'Creative Imagination' in Our Age"), for attending to "the self-forgotten incarnation process of the world," rather than to "the stylistic certainty of appearances" (*CP* 75-79; 76; also in *Metropolitan Icons* 151-59; 153). An English translation of JP's essay, by John Batki, will be found in *Modern Poetry in Translation*, no. 11 (Autumn 1971) 13-14. Cf. also "Metronome," lines 1-2.

Lines 6-7 "your city / the eternal city": Budapest or Rome? Probably the former, but the formulation is not without interest. Cf. the notes on "White Pietà" and "Metropolitan Icons."

Lines 11-12: cf. Ezra Pound's dictum: "'Literature is news that stays news.'" See Ezra Pound, *ABC of Reading*, The New Classics Series (Norfolk, CT: New Directions, n.d. [1951]) 29 (with "stays" in all capitals).

Line 13 "Scribe": literal rendition of the Hungarian *írnok*, a somewhat archaic equivalent for "journalist," "reporter," hence "writer" favored by JP; cf. line 2 of "Betűk, sorok" ("Letters, Lines") (*CP* 123). That these equivalents deservedly applied to JP and that he was aware of that, is clear also from the impressive feuilletonistic writing he had been doing for *Új Ember* since 1 November 1957 (and subsequently gathered in *Nail & Oil* and in *Nadir*).

"Gallows in Winter" (94; 131)

A: *Splinters* 28.

Comment: *Convv.* 159-60, with recitation of poem.

Imagery: cf. "For Jutta," section "*Letter*."

Line 2 "Who lead him up?" (grammar): English "Who leads him up?" can have either a singular or plural answer; the less usual rendition chosen here is meant to indicate JP's insistence on the plural.

Line 3, stockyard versus gallows: in line 1 of "Passion" the distinction is blurred, if only because "the butcher's assistants" (line 4) have just slain "the Lamb" (animal image, human and divine reality; presence implied in title of poem). In "Gallows in Winter," the distinction is restored.

Line 4 "Who kills and whom?": cf. the poem "Ki és kit?" ("Who and Whom?") (*CP* 115), especially with its image "Just like a lit-up / gallows, ..." (lines 4-5).

Line 10 "Gallows in winter": distinctively not one of the winter landscapes of Brueghel, an artist whose work JP admired (see only *Convv*. 80, 197), nor indeed the landscape in Sándor Petőfi's poem "A puszta, télen" ("The Puszta, in Winter"), both conceptions full of life. Behind JP's conception is a metaphysical winter; cf. "that final oblivion / that the Father will send upon the world" ("For Jutta," section "*Letter*," lines 4-5).

Line 10 "We know nothing": refers us to JP's views on knowledge. Only the ignorant truly know, and vice versa. Cf. "Experience," lines 3-5.

"Van Gogh's Prayer" (95-96; 133)

A: *Vigilia* 36, no. 12 (December 1971): 814.

Comment: *Nadir* 1:422-23; *Convv*. 232-33 (with recitation of poem); Kuklay 272-74 (272-73: quotes essay in *Nadir*; see below). Tüskés 211.

Title: see JP's article "Van Gogh kiállítás Párizsban" ("Van Gogh Exhibition in Paris") (*Nadir* 1:422-23), especially 422: "No one in modern painting ever *prayed* as he did. His art, however, is religious not thematically, but *within all of itself.*" The article dates from 2 April 1972. Further (422): "Van Gogh makes us a gift of what is ours. Of a tree branch, a shoe, a chair stood in front of a window." For such concern with objects elsewhere in JP's writing, see "Apocrypha," 1.30 and 2.40. For comment by JP on Van Gogh, see *Convv*. 136, 173; on Van Gogh, see also the notes on "Van Gogh," "The Henchman's Room," and "Metronome."

Lines 3, 5, 6, 7, 8, 10, 11: probably subjects of paintings that JP saw at the Paris exhibition.

"Every Breath" (96; 135)
A: *Splinters* 34.
Line 1 "Every breath": Cf. "Admonition," line 1 "Not breathing."
Lines 3-4, images of sea and wave: see the note on "Meetings."
Lines 9-10, similes: they are explained by JP's situs as poet (see the note on line 11).
Line 11 "God's tranquil happiness": what is eternal is, paradoxically, depicted in the poem as earned. The explanation is that JP is a poet and, like Dante, he can conjure eternity only under the sign of what is not eternity. JP knew his Dante, most probably in the translation by Mihály Babits. For JP's brief tribute to the "celestial geometry" and "scholastic beauty" of the *Commedia*, see *Nadir* 1:133 (in the article "Az idő sürgetése" ["The Urging of Time"], *Nadir* 1:132-34).

"The Rest Is Mercy" (96; 137)
A: *Vigilia* 36, no. 12 (December 1971): 814.
Comment: Kuklay 150-51; S. Radnóti 83-84. Kuklay associates the poem with JP's late essay "Keresztről keresztre" ("From Cross to Cross") (*Nadir* 1:508-10), which dates from 28 October 1979.
Lines 1-2, metaphors: autobiographical (on JP and his father, see Tüskés 45-46).
Lines 3-4, images of corridor and of opening land: cf. "Four-Liner."
Line 7: cf. Miklós Radnóti, "Fourth Eclogue," line 48 "earth, deep with memory, will lay you to rest" (*MR* 249). On the older poet, see JP's article "Radnóti Miklós" (*Nadir* 1:460-62; appeared in *Élet és Irodalom* [Life and Letters], 2 November 1974). On MR, see also Pomogáts and Sanders.

"Meetings" (99; 139)

A: *Kortárs* 15, no. 11 (November 1971): 1725; also

Új Írás 11, no. 12 (December 1971): 58.

Dedicatee: Júlia Szilágyi (b. 1938), applied artist, textile designer, close friend of JP since the second half of the 1960s. On Szilágyi, see *Nadir* 1:419-20 (with text of "Meetings," 420).

Title: cf. "A mi napunk" ("Our Day") (*CP* 115), line 8 "találkozhat" ("can meet").

Comment: Kuklay 235-36; S. Radnóti 90-91; *Convv*. 182-99, interview "'Eljuthatunk a derűig'" ("'We Can Attain to Good Cheer'"), which is mostly on musical experience. According to S. Radnóti, the theme of "Meetings" is good cheer, also ecstasy.

Line 3 "Wave with wave": cf. "Every Breath," line 3: "Strange that the sea should be deathless"; also the juxtaposition of sea with love in "A tengerpartra" ("On the Seashore") (*CP* 28), and in "Egy szenvedély margójára" ("On the Margin of a Passion") (*CP* 29), with the latter's opening image of a small child walking on the seashore and looking for pebbles. On JP's early postwar experience of the sea, see Tüskés 108-09 (Italian trip).

"The Seventh Circle of Hell" (99; 141)

A: *Új Írás* 11, no. 12 (December 1971): 58.

Title: A Dantean conceit; on JP's awareness of and response to Dante, see *Nadir* 2:226 (but five index entries); also the note on "Every Breath." On the theme of hell elsewhere in JP's poetry, see "Without Witnesses," "Spaces," and "Infernó" (*CP* 125).

The number 7: cf. "KZ Oratorio," Young Boy: "There are seven cubes" (64, 9; 83, 2). Dante's Inferno has nine circles: but see the importance of the number 7 in Revelation (from the candlesticks to the seals).

Lines 6-7: cf. "Through a Lifetime," closing lines; also lines 6-9 of "Zsolozsma" ("Psalm") (*CP* 123).

Line 8: addresses a woman, the beloved with whom the poet has had such an impossible relationship. Cf. the notes on "Love's Desert," "Apocrypha," and "Four-Liner."

"Through a Lifetime" (100; 143)

A: *Új Írás* 11, no. 12 (December 1971): 59, without the dedication.

Dedicatee: JP's brother-in-law, Dr. Barnabás Kovács (1912-1971), husband of JP's sister, Veronika (Erika), née Pilinszky (1919-1976), and father of Dr. Péter Kovács. See Tüskés 13 (photo of brother-in-law and his wife). To his sister JP inscribed his poem "Rongyaidban és kitakarva" ("In Your Rags and Uncovered") (*CP* 97) and, to her memory, *Conversations with Sheryl Sutton* (on the latter, see the note on "Crime and Punishment").

Comment: S. Radnóti 77.

Section 1, the havoc we wreak in our human relationships: related in theme to "The Seventh Circle of Hell" (see also below).

2.4-5 "the world's / immaculate and primeval cloth": an allusion to Christ's robe and his other garments (Matthew 27:35; Mark 15:24; Luke 23:34; John 19:23-24).

4.2, both kinds of sleep: cf. "The Seventh Circle of Hell," line 7.

"Looking for the Prodigal Son" (102; 145)

A: *Splinters* 48.

Title and theme: Jesus' parable of the Prodigal Son (Luke 15:11-32), sounded in "Apocrypha," 2.11-12. Luke 15:24: "he was lost, and is found" (also 15:32).

Comment: Kuklay 24-25. Kuklay juxtaposes text of poem with a passage from the essay "From Cross to Cross" (*Nadir* 1:508-10).

Theme: The theme of the Prodigal Son (and of "prodigal son-hood") is one of JP's most important. See *Nadir* 2:235 (index); "From a Lyrist's Diary," dated 12 November 1972 (not in *Nadir*: see Kuklay 19-20); and the poem "Tékozlók" ("Prodigals") (*CP* 141-42).

Line 3 "Our son": present and not present simultaneously, like Dulcinea in *Don Quixote*, or Nachodine in *Wilhelm Meisters Wanderjahre*.

Lines 3-5, the son among houses, visual effect: the passage strongly conjures Dürer's copperplate engraving of 1496, *The Prodigal Son amid the Swine*; see Walter L. Strauss (ed.), *The Intaglio Prints of Albrecht Dürer: Engravings, Etchings and Drypoints*, 2nd ed. (New York: Kennedy Galleries and Abaris Books, 1977) 45 (pl. 11), and 44 (commentary). Strauss 44 (quoting "1778 Hüsgen 29"): "It is generally considered to be a self-portrait." JP's own lines on the Prodigal Son also constitute an act of self-portraiture ("Apocrypha"). Both of JP's portrayals answer to Dürer's, "one of the most tender and at the same time most sorrowful of [his] conceptions" (Strauss 44, quoting his source, "1869 Heaton, p. 189"). That JP makes no mention of Dürer anywhere in his prose writings is, to say the least, surprising. He speaks of Bosch, Brueghel, Cranach, and other artists of the Renaissance and early modern periods (see *Nadir*, index), but not of Dürer.

Line 8, together with entire conception of poem: This may have in its background the "Quaerens me" stanza from the "Dies Irae" of Thomas à Celano. We can assume that JP was familiar with the poem, but in its musical setting, as a part of the "Recordare" movement in Mozart's *Requiem in D Minor, K. 626*, he would have been reminded of the stanza often. The one musical element in the film script *Requiem* is Mozart's work, heard at one point on the radio (see *Nadir* 2:36).

"Cattle Brand" (102; 147)
A: *Splinters* 49.
Comment: Kuklay 119.

2.1: "the world," meaning humanity, people, possibly a carry-over from French *le monde*. Cf. Hölderlin, "Der Einzige," third version, lines 71-72 "Nemlich immer jauchzet die Welt / Hinweg von dieser Erde, ..." (Hanser 1:469).

2.2-3: This is the condition of post-Holocaust humanity—the Holocaust is the universal Crucifixion.

"The Way Only" (106-07; 149)
A: *Splinters* 65.
Comment: Kuklay 151-52 (a Darwinian interpretation of lines 3-7).

Lines 1 "Evening Mass," 2 "elevation of the Host," 7 "wolves," 8 "monstrance": cf. "For Jutta," section "*January*"; also "KZ Oratorio," M. R.'s, the young girl's, tale of the pure-hearted wolf. See also the notes there.

"Enough" (109-10; 151)
A: *Splinters* 73.
Comment: Kuklay 233-34; S. Radnóti 100-03 (103: quotes text whole).
Lines 1-2: cf. "Spaces" and other poems in which spatial imagery dominates.
Line 2 "pigpen": cf. "Apocrypha," 1.4 "the silence of the kennels"; also "Love's Desert," line 12 "boarded-up chicken coops"; "Celebration of Nadir," line 1 "the bloodstained warmth of the barns," and the notes on all three.
Line 3, catalogue, and its relevance to lines 1-2: cf. JP's statement in an interview: "I believe we should ... strive ... to let [the cosmos] come all the way to our threshold, ... For in that case [i.e., once we have done that] the objects in the universe point beyond themselves and mirror that something that we cannot have a view of" (*Convv.* 197-98).
Lines 5 "someone steps in," 7 "a face, a presence": according to S. Radnóti, "Enough" is a key poem on the principle of presence. Cf. JP's interview with Mátyás Domokos, "A költői jelenlét" ("Poetic Presence") (*Convv.* 91-110).
Stanza 3, images of socializing, forgetting, acceptance: Kuklay juxtaposes the text of the poem with an excerpt from JP's interview with István Szigeti, "'We Can Attain to Good Cheer'" (*Convv.* 182-99). Particularly suggestive is Szigeti's question on friendship, and how JP fields it, with the Cranach-Brueghel passage (196-98). Cf. note on line 3.

"Straight Labyrinth" (110; 153)
A: *Splinters* 74.
Comment: *Convv.* 182-99, the interview with István Szigeti, with its somewhat bittersweet, semi-pessimistic title (JP recites poem, 198-99); Kuklay 284-86. The latter juxtaposes text of poem with an excerpt from JP's essay "Az idő sürgetése" ("The Urging of Time") (*Nadir* 1:132-34; dated 4 March 1962).

Stress is placed on union, in love, on meeting (cf. poem "Meetings" above).

Title and theme: On "labyrinth," see *Nadir* 2:233 (index); also the interview with László Krassó, "A labirintus járatai" ("Paths of the Labyrinth") (*Convv.* 209-15).

Lines 5-6 "a set table / where there is no first and no last guest": cf. Jesus' parable of the marriage of the king's son (Matthew 22:2-14).

from *Dénouement* (1974)

"Two Portraits" (113-14; 157)

A: *Dénouement* 8.

Joint dedicatees: "For Mari and Gyuszi": Mari Törőcsik (see the note on "Holy Thief"), and her husband, the film director Gyula Maár (b. 1934). On Törőcsik and Maár, see also the interview with Sándor Forgács titled "Egy színházi este" ("An Evening in the Theater"), in which JP reports on the Győr premiere of Ernő Szép's play *Patika* (Pharmacy), directed by Maár, with Törőcsik in the principal role (*Convv.* 179-81). See also the interview with GyM, "Pilinszky-portré a televízióban" ("P. Portrait on Television") (*Convv.* 219-41).

Section "*Brontë*": Refers to Emily Brontë's novel *Wuthering Heights*; the work, in the translation by István Sőtér (Budapest: Európa, 1962), was one of JP's most important literary experiences. (Information kindly provided by Dr. Péter Kovács in a letter.) On Emily Brontë, see *Convv.* 50.

Images in this section: cf. "Infernó" (*CP* 125), with its catalogue of household properties.

Section "*Rembrandt*": Kuklay (196-97) juxtaposes these four lines with JP's article "300 esztendeje" ("It Has Been 300 Years") (*Nadir* 1:380; dated 19 October 1969), commemorating the tercentenary of Rembrandt's death.

Lines 1 and 2 "of ashes and vinegar": the repeated phrase refers to Rembrandt's palette; in the essay JP writes that R worked "with his yellowish-brown ashen colors" (*Nadir* 1:380, quoted in Kuklay 197).

Lines 1 and 2, subjects of paintings, "Paternal house"; "Kiss and handkiss":

in contrast with our Dürer problem (see the note on "Looking for the Prodigal Son"), here I would rather not attempt to identify these images with specific paintings. The two subjects, when taken together, suggest the Prodigal Son theme once again, one R treated a number of times, and in several media. His painting on the subject is, however, one that JP could at most have seen as a color reproduction in a book; it is in the Hermitage Museum, St. Petersburg. See Christian Tümpel and Astrid Tümpel (authors and eds.), *Rembrandt* (n.p. [Paris:] Albin Michel, 1986) 359 (color plate of *Le Retour de l'Enfant Prodigue,* c. 1666-1669, oil on canvas).

Line 4 "in a discipline beyond death": a characteristically terse tribute to the survival of the work. Well may it strike us as almost ironic, in view of the downsizing of R's oeuvre we are witnessing in our day.

"Opening" (114; 159)

A: *Dénouement* 9.

Comment: Kuklay 239-43; juxtaposes text with two essays by JP: "From a Lyrist's Diary" (*Nadir* 1:458-59; dated 8 September 1974) and "Egyetlen pillanat kegyelme" ("A Single Moment's Grace") (*Nadir* 1:287-89), both of them disquisitions on younger years, and on dream.

Line 1 "Childhood's alchemy": one of JP's most important concerns. Cf. "Self-Portrait from 1944," "Auschwitz," "Sketch," not last reminiscences of the institution he visited as a child (see *Convv.* 128-29; also our note on "Miss I. B.").

Line 3 "the untouched gates": cf. "Harbach 1944," stanza 8, also line 18.

Line 4 "the sluice system of dream": the ball bearings and gears of surrealist vision. The fact that "sluice system" suggests watery passage between consciousness and dream again conjures Dante, particularly the opening lines of *Purgatorio.*

The poem as a whole: It treats of approaching death, a theme all of the poems share. In this JP differs from Miklós Radnóti only in that his expectation transpires in a religious rather than in a political context.

238

"Game" (114; 161)

A: *Dénouement* 10.

Title: Dr. Kovács tells me that the game of billiards did not hold any particular attraction for JP's father. The image serves the purposes of the poem only. The latter depicts a confidence trickster's metaphysical game; this is the game of billiards that is not one, the *x* that is not *x*. Cf., e.g., "Van Gogh's Prayer," stanza 3.

Line 2 "my dead father": on the death of JP's father, whose name was also János Pilinszky (1886-1937), see Tüskés 19, 44-46.

Lines 5-8 "gravesite"–"man-back" metaphor: Kuklay (144) quotes an excerpt from *Conversations with Sheryl Sutton* inclusive of the image; the passage is about JP's father (chap. 1; *Nadir* 2:127-28). On the metaphor itself, see the note on "Afterword."

Lines 11-15, image of billiard balls: cf. "A Little Night Music," section "*Midnight*," line 5 "the motionless billiard balls"; cf. also "Van Gogh," 2.3 "sun" and 2.5 "iron ball," and the note on "Miss I. B." "Van Gogh" immediately precedes "A Little Night Music."

Line 17 "I too halt":   or will soon. Cf. "Sketch," closing line: "I'm perishing."

"Definition" (116; 163)

A: *Kortárs* 16, no. 11 (November 1972):   1804.

Comment: Kuklay 16-20.

Line 1 "To be a worm": cf. Goethe, *Faust I*, "Nacht": "Ein furchtsam weggekrümmter Wurm" (line 498) is Erdgeist's definition of the missing Faust in Faust (494 "Wo bist du, Faust ... ?"). Faust's present state satisfies the terms of JP's definition ("Definition," lines 2-9, everything from the craving of a glance [lines 3-5] to the burrowing in [lines 6-9]).

If JP read Goethe's play, which he most probably did, it may well have been in the translation by László Kálnoky. See Goethe, *Faust, Válogatott művei* (Selected Works [in 5 vols.]), *Drámák* 2 (Budapest: Európa, 1963 [in the same volume: *Urfaust*, trans. Zoltán Jékely; *Faust II*, trans. György Sárközi]).   On Goethe, see *Nadir* 1:170, 313 (mention in passing, not pertinent to *Faust*).

With the worm motif in line 1 of "Definition," cf. "To Two Lovers," and "In memoriam N. N." (*CP* 31-32), lines 22, 34.

"Experience" (116; 165)

A: *Kortárs* 16, no. 11 (November 1972): 1804.

Comment: Kuklay 163-67; S. Radnóti 124-25 (125: quotes lines 1-5), theme of "new nakedness," "inarticulateness," of the ignorance of omniscience, and vice versa. S. Radnóti calls this final stage of JP's art the "birth of a new primitivism" (125).

Lines 1-2, Kronos aphorism; as the old Hungarian saying goes: "The revolution eats its children." Here the mythic image refers to JP's Platonic distinction between "facts" and "reality." In other words: experience, empirical science, "devours" the laws whose formulation it encourages; it is an ongoing process (see Kuklay 164).

Lines 3-4 "Genuine knowledge / is inexperienced": see S. Radnóti, as above, and the note on "Gallows in Winter," line 10.

Lines 7-8 "when / the henchman snacks on bacon": cf. "The Henchman's Room," line 1.

"Stavrogin Says Goodbye" (123; 167)

A: *Dénouement* 39.

Title: There is more on the Dostoyevskian reference in the note on "Stavrogin Returns" below; full citation to the novel will be found there as well. Stavrogin "says goodbye" before going to Switzerland (at end of novel).

Comment: Kuklay 60-61.

Line 5 "a single rose": a single human life, of incomparable preciousness and fragility. It is a part of the narrative in *The Devils* (*The Possessed*) that the "devils" kill one of their own ranks (Shatov; see pt. 3, chap. 5, sec. 3 [Penguin 578]: "Kirilov knew nothing about the decision to murder Shatov, ...").

"Jewel" (124; 169)

A: *Békés megyei Népújság* (B. County People's News), 27 January 1974.

Comment: Kuklay 35-36; juxtaposes text of poem with essay by JP, "Napfogyatkozás" ("Solar Eclipse") (*Nadir* 1:441; dated 17 June 1973). Analogy between "mirror" of fashion and vanity and the state of the individual who, sitting at a richly laden table, will forever remain hungry. Cf. Plato's view of the ultimate condition of the tyrannical man (*Republic* 579d-e [Shorey]).

Lines 2, 3, 4, 5, 7 grammar (pronouns): since Hungarian is genderless in its third-person singular pronouns (*ő* "he, she"; *az* "it"), JP's poem cannot give us an idea through the use of pronouns alone of whether a male or female antelope is intended. But I believe it is clear that, in vivid contrast to "Dream" (see below), the antelope in "Jewel" is far from genderless, and that she is indeed female. JP's thinking on the matter predates, to say the least, radical feminist views. Images in lines 1-3 (jeweled being admiring self in a mirror) and 6 ("giving birth") leave no doubts as to gender.

"After Confession" (124; 171)

A: *Új Írás* 13, no. 9 (September 1973): 12.

Comment: JP's article "Three Meetings" (*Nadir* 1:295-97; dated 25 December 1965), with its three subheadings "Paul Klee," "Dürrenmatt," "Valsainte"; Koppány and Kocsis; Kuklay 250-54; Tüskés 199-201 (on trip to Switzerland, with photos, by JP: of Dürrenmatt, 198; of Weöres, with Carthusian monk at Valsainte, 199; of cemetery of Valsainte monastery, 200).

Kuklay (252) quotes prose on Dostoyevsky as discovered by JP as a twelve-year-old (excerpt from "'Good Cheer'" interview with István Szigeti, see *Convv.* 185-86); preceding this, Kuklay (251) quotes from *The Devils*.

Line 6 "the strong murderers," especially as followed by line 8 "women" and "infants": is this an allusion to Oskar Kokoschka's expressionist play *Mörder, Hoffnung der Frauen* (1909)? Could JP have read it, or attended a performance?

"Infinitive" (125; 173)

A: *Új Írás* 13, no. 9 (September 1973): 12.

Comment: Kuklay 222.

   Title: more attention to grammar; cf. "Imperfect Tense," "Van Gogh," and "Hasonlat" ("Simile") (*CP* 95), with its infinitives.

   Theme: powerful anti-war, anti-violence statement (see also below).

   Language: The following version of the translation, one I weighed at first, contains no infinitives with *to*, but it is tighter:

> You can still open it.
> And lock him up.
> You can still string him up.
> And cut him down.
> You can still give him birth.
> And shovel him under.

Problem of gender: cf. "Jewel." In "Infinitive," the poet mourns mothers' sons, taken away and killed in war or other senseless violence.

"Poem" (125; 175)

A: *Tiszatáj* (Tisza Region) 28, no. 1 (January 1974): 23.

Comment: Kuklay 178-84; S. Radnóti 91-92.

   Lines 5-8, syntax: in the original, predicate nominative followed by subject. In translation I invert this, otherwise I would have to write: "God is what God is."

   Lines 9-10: Kuklay's lengthy analysis comments on Theodor W. Adorno's dictum on the impossibility of poetry after Auschwitz, and quotes (180) from JP's inteview with László Krassó, "A labirintus járatai" ("Paths of the Labyrinth") (*Convv.* 209-15; 211-12), among other texts.

   "Poem" is, once again, an eloquent contribution to the Holocaust poetry. This is particularly evident from the poem's structure; while all nine of its sentences are of the form "predicate nominative equals (else: does not equal) subject" (see also above), only the ninth and final sentence occupies two lines.

It is an exfoliation of the first eight.

"Stavrogin Returns" (126; 177)

A: *Dénouement* 49.

Title: The allusion to Dostoyevsky's novel *The Devils* (*The Possessed*) is clear from the title of the poem alone. JP probably read it in the translation by Imre Makai: Dosztojevszkij, *Ördögök* (Devils) (Budapest: Magyar Helikon, 1972). Below we cite: Fyodor Dostoyevsky, *The Devils* (*The Possessed*), trans., with an Introduction, by David Magarshack (London, New York: Penguin Books, 1953, rpt. 1971 [18th prtg. 1991]). Cited as Penguin and page.

Comment: Kuklay 61-63. Kuklay (62-63) quotes from *The Devils* portions of pt. 2, chap. 7, sec. 2 ("At Virginsky's" [Penguin 405]) and pt. 2, chap. 8 ("Ivan the Crown-Prince" [Penguin 418-19]) (lecture by the "lame teacher," on Shigalyov's "theory of equality").

Kuklay's interpretation of the text of JP's poem is brilliant. But it does not take account of the important point that Stavrogin himself should be considered one of those "mounted butterflies." He too "commits what is forbidden," responsible as he is for the death of his wife (Penguin 666) and of the little girl, Matryosha (on the latter's suicide, see "Stavrogin's Confession" [Penguin 671-704; 687-93]). As Kuklay too notes, returning to Russia from Switzerland, Stavrogin himself commits suicide by hanging (Penguin 668-69, very end of novel).

Lines 7-8, repeated occurrence of "glisten": cf. "Afterword," line 32 "Gleam—in vain!" and the note there.

On Dostoyevsky in JP's work, see also the poem "In memoriam F. M. Dostoyevsky" (*CP* 122); also *Nadir* 2:226 (index); *Convv.* 79; and Tüskés 177, 179 (with portrait, 176). See also the notes on the poems "Belated Grace," "Under a Portrait," "Elysium in November," "Crime and Punishment," "Stavrogin Says Goodbye," and "Miss I. B."

from *Crater* (1976)

"Auschwitz" (130; 181)

A: *Crater* 194.

Dedicatee: Erzsébet Schaár (1908-1975), distinguished Hungarian sculptor (*MÉL*). Works by her are reproduced on the cover of JP, *Crater*, trans. Peter Jay (see Bibliography). On Schaár, see also Tüskés 182: "When the poet's nephew, the art historian Péter Kovács, receives an appointment at the István Király Múzeum [King Stephen Museum] at Székesfehérvár, one after another he organizes exhibits of the best of contemporary Hungarian visual artists."

Comment: Kuklay 185-90. Quotes such an essay as "Oswiecim"; also a piece not in *Nadir* or in *Nail & Oil*: "Schaár Erzsébet kiállításának megnyitója" ("Opening of Exhibition of E. S.") (dated Székesfehérvár, István Csók Gallery, 23 June 1974) (Kuklay 189).

Kuklay (84-86) recommends that we compare "Auschwitz" with "Szakitás" ("Breaking Off") (*CP* 141); cf. also "Önarckép 1944-ből" ("Self-Portrait from 1944") (*CP* 73) and "Önarckép 1974" ("Self-Portrait 1974") (*CP* 129).

"Spaces" (130; 183)

A: *Crater* 194-95.

Comment: Kuklay 53-57: good interpretation (53). In addition, "Spaces" may have something to do with Hugo von Hofmannsthal's poem "Manche freilich ..." (see *Die Gedichte und kleinen Dramen* ... [Leipzig: Insel, 1911] 16). By HvH, JP translated a portion of his play *Elektra* (*CP* 211-14); the translation appeared in the July 1946 issue (vol. 1, no. 1) of *Újhold* (58-62; see *CP* 254; also Tüskés 98-99, 101).

Lines 14-15 "that / sole being whom I love": cf. "Love's Desert," and the note there.

"Dream" (131; 185)

A: *Crater* 196.

Comment: Kuklay 163, who holds that the "genderless being" of line 1 is an angel, one who kisses the poet on the forehead, so that "you cannot see its eyes" (line 8). For an alternative reading, see below.

Line 1 "The genderless being": with this being, and its beauty (lines 3, 5, 7), cf. "Gothic," lines 2-3.

Line 4 "a presidential election": this suggests proximity of the date of composition of "Dream" to JP's visit to the United States in the summer of 1975. The presidential election campaign that Jimmy Carter won was but six months away, and already in the air. As far as JP's concept of the "genderless being" is concerned, see his article "Amerikai képeslap" ("Postcard from America") (*Nadir* 1:467-71; dated 6 July 1975). In it (469-70), he writes about the American airline "stewardesses," "rather like schoolgirls" (470; also trained to be impersonal, hence "genderless"). They seem to have sponsored the image of the beautiful "genderless being," who leans over the poet (implied in lines 7-8), just as airline attendants often lean over passengers they are helping, so that indeed you cannot see their eyes (line 8). JP may also be thinking of Dezső Kosztolányi's 1926 novel *Édes Anna*; reading it now, in the new translation by George Szirtes (New York: New Directions, 1993), may help one understand what a mid-European writer might mean by a "beautiful genderless being."

For more on "genderless being," see the poem "Sírkövemre" ("On My Gravestone") (*CP* 115), line 3 "Te szegény, szegény nemtelen lény" ("You poor, poor genderless being").

"Two" (131; 187)

A: *Crater* 196.

Comment: Kuklay 101-03 (connects poem with the classic experiment with pendulums, demonstrating laws of gravitation, carried out by Lóránd Eötvös).

Lines 1-2: Besides the experiment, with weights, Kuklay connects the

245

poem with JP's essay "Amikor imádkozunk" ("When We Pray") (not in *Nadir*; dated 4 February 1973). The essay stresses polar contrasts, as do lines 1-2. Line 3: one of numerous such paradoxes in JP's poetry. In contrast to "Van Gogh's Prayer," line 9 ("where I too lived and do not live"), however, here a causal element is introduced. "I am because I am not" makes us overhear the Cartesian "I think, therefore I am." Unfortunately, JP is silent on René Descartes; on another seventeenth-century figure, see "Pascal" (*CP* 129).

"Hölderlin" (134; 189)

A: *Kortárs* 18, no. 9 (September 1974): 1349.

Dedicatee: György Kurtág (b. 1926), major Hungarian composer. He set four of JP's poems to music; see *Négy dal Pilinszky János verseire / ... / Four Songs to Poems by János Pilinszky*, opus 11, score 16841 (Vienna: Universal Edition; Budapest: Editio Musica, 1979). The poems are "Alkohol" ("Alcohol") (*CP* 122); "In memoriam F. M. Dostoyevsky" (*CP* 122); "Hölderlin"; and "Verés" ("Beating") (*CP* 133). See also the Introduction, and n. 25.

Title: For JP, Hölderlin was a major experience. See *Nadir* 2:227 (index); also the rather lengthy disquisition on Hölderlin—by the interviewer—in the interview with Mátyás Domokos, "Poetic Presence" (*Convv.* 98-99). Domokos's choice of allusions in Hölderlin's proximity to the lyric dictions of Apollinaire and of Dylan Thomas (99) appears indebted to the Afterword, by Mihály Sükösd, to the translated edition of Hölderlin's works and letters edited by István Bernáth (Budapest: Magyar Helikon, 1961 [529]). This is suggestive; JP's own awareness of Hölderlin may well be renewed by acquaintance with this volume (in addition to his having used the one-volume Insel edition in school days; see the note on the Hölderlin problem in "Apocrypha," section 2).

Comment: Kuklay (167) juxtaposes JP's "Hölderlin" with Lőrinc Szabó's translation of Hölderlin's early Frankfurt ode "An die Parzen" (Hanser 1:188). JP most probably knew Szabó's translation, by the time he wrote his own poem, from the collected shorter translations: Szabó Lőrinc, *Örök barátaink* (Our Eternal Friends), ed. Mátyás Domokos, 2 vols. (Budapest: Szépirodalmi, 1958), 1:590. He may also have known the version by György Rónay, available in book form since 1943 (in Franklin's bilingual selection of poems by Novalis and Hölderlin, ed. and trans. György Rónay [75]). If so, the latter may have appealed to him more; Szabó's jauntily upbeat ending, with a question, seems inappropriate to the tone and ethos of Hölderlin's lyric conception.

Lines 1-2: they bear allusions besides the longed-for success in poetic creativity expressed in "An die Parzen." There are intimations of personal tragedy, disappointments, failures, presumed (and since contested) insanity. Among a vast literature, see only Pierre Bertaux, *Friedrich Hölderlin* (Frankfurt am Main: Suhrkamp, 1978).

Line 3 "What have I not been?": along with the foregoing, this carries ideas on the rise of Hölderlin's star as an early modern, on how critics since 1913 have seen the poet.

Line 3 "Gladly I'll die": to be resurrected, not last by poets and other artists who have addressed Hölderlin in their work. With JP's homage, cf. two other Hungarian Hölderlin poems: those by Sándor Weöres and by László Nagy. Kurtág's composition also reminds us of the *Six Hölderlin Fragments* of Benjamin Britten, as well as of cyclic Hölderlin compositions by Hanns Eisler and by Paul Hindemith.

"Green" (134; 191)

A: *Kortárs* 18, no. 9 (September 1974): 1349.

Comment: Kuklay 154.

Title: A rare poem on nature.

Text: On people as "wood," see Kuklay, juxtaposition (144): "Mother ... was a grove, a school of trees to her death ..." (from *Conversations with Sheryl Sutton*). Cf. Hölderlin, "Die Eichbäume" (Hanser 1:180-81), which JP may be remembering either in the translation by György Rónay (Lyra Mundi ed. 18-19) or in that by István Bernáth (1961, 62).

Line 4 "tree": cf. "Kopogtatás" ("Knocking") (*CP* 142); also *Convv.* 172.

"Earthen Vessel" (134; 193)

A: *Forrás* (Source), February 1975: 26. *

Title and conception: Burning contrast with biological "Green"; shows JP's keen sense for the poetic suggestivities of color.

Comment: Kuklay 103-96 (juxtaposes text with religious prose).

Lines 2-3, simile: suggests a double image. By the time the poet and his reader "see" the ceramic vessel, it is hard and cool. Nevertheless, the poet sees himself as being inside the kiln, at the time of firing.

"Gothic" (135; 195)

A: *Crater* 201.

Comment: Kuklay 267-70.

Line 1 "The creeper-crawler": cf. "Definition," line 1 "To be a worm: what does that mean?" In "Gothic," JP seems to be giving this lowly creature a bit more credit than before; the "worm" is back to its status as a human. The capacity to behold beauty is an important point the poem makes.

Line 1 "under the spell": *pace* Kuklay, the "creeper-crawler" could not possibly fall into the beautiful being's hair and still behold her beauty (lines 1-3). This is a patent impossibility; to see anything, we need our physical distance from it. We have it as we behold the interior of a Gothic cathedral, and are made to feel like a "tiny green caterpillar" (Kuklay 267).

Line 2 "your shoulder-cascading hair": JP's vision has clear affinity with Rembrandt's etching *Girl with Hair Falling on Her Shoulders (The Great Jewish Bride)*, as in: Yevgeny Levitin, *Rembrandt, Etchings*, Introduction and catalogue, trans. Andrew Baratt, The Collection of the Pushkin Museum of Fine Arts, Moscow (Leningrad: Aurora Art Publishers, 1973), pl. 29, cat. no. 162 (223). Cf. the Rembrandt problem touched on in the note on "Two Portraits."

Lines 2-3: Who is the creature with "your shoulder-cascading hair" and with "your incorruptible, doomed perfection"? Certainly not a "genderless" one ("Dream"), nor indeed an animal ("Jewel"); rather, a woman, perhaps the moment's beloved.

Line 3 "your incorruptible, doomed perfection": cf. James Joyce, *Portrait of the Artist as a Young Man*, chap. 4 (end): "and touched with the wonder of

248

mortal beauty, her face" (Viking Portable ed. [⁴1952] 432). JP was quite aware of Joyce, despite one, somewhat disparaging, remark on him (*Nadir* 1:430, in a comparison with Dostoyevsky).

The poem establishes an effective parallel between the "imperishable, doomed perfection" of line 3 and the Gothic church of the closing line. Both are "models of the All." The parallel, even metaphoric relation, between the body and a building is not new; cf. the exhortation by Saint Paul: "What? know ye not that your body is the temple of the Holy Ghost ... ?" (1 Corinthians 6:19).

"Crater" (136; 197)
A: *Új Írás* 14, no. 10 (October 1974): 12.
Comment: Kuklay 103-08.

Line 3 "You": this could not possibly be a woman (as Kuklay claims). Even stylistic parallels (Tüskés 236-37) cannot connect "Crater" to the Jutta experience. The "you" of line 3 could only be a male friend. Cf. "Elysium in November," where the comparison with Alyosha Karamazov resolves the issue of gender.

Line 2 "In a cigar store. At an auction": A woman of JP's day could visit either place of business, but she would be less likely to do so than a man.

Stanza 2, poiesis of standstill, of frustrated movement: in JP's poetic world this is as important as it is in Franz Kafka's. JP on Kafka: see *Nadir* 1:398-99.

Lines 6-7: cf. T. S. Eliot, "Burnt Norton," which JP undoubtedly knew in the translation by István Vas. Kuklay (98) quotes "Burnt Norton," 2.16-21 and 24-26, with Eliot's lines 24-25 telescoped into one in Vas. See T. S. Eliot, *The Complete Poems and Plays* (New York: Harcourt Brace, 1952) 118-20; 119. Eliot's lines 18-20, seen by JP in Hungarian translation, could have given him the idea here for his own Heraclitean lines 6-7.

Lines 9-10: cf. "Harbach 1944," stanza 4. The "tailgating" and movement without movement also remind us of the purposeless motions and existence of Raskolnikov in *Crime and Punishment*.

Lines 11-12: these two lines could support the woman image urged by Kuklay, but do not necessarily do so. Someone "reproaching me for my birth" could have other points in mind, especially in the Hungary of JP's day: wartime anti-Semitism, else Stalinist discrimination against one of *értelmiségi* (intellectual, white-collar) background. It *can* imply unwillingness to marry someone because of birth, but it need not. Not to mention that "birth" did not prevent tens of thousands of racially mixed marriages, even in the worst of times.

"Miss I. B." (143; 199)

A: *Tiszatáj* 28, no. 12 (December 1974): 40.

Comment: *Convv.* 229-30; Kuklay 208-12; Tüskés 26-31 (on the biographical background).

Title: "I. B." is an invented set of initials; it is also certain that its similarity to line 4 "Iron Ball" is pure coincidence. JP knew no English, and the Hungarian equivalent of "Iron Ball" is "Vasgolyó." These initials also have nothing to do with the dedication of the poem "Felelet" ("Reply") (*CP* 105) to "*I. B.*" This, Dr. Kovács tells me, is the filmmaker Ingmar Bergman, whose work JP deeply admired. (On Bergman, see *Nadir* 1:231-32 and 520-23.)

Genre and tone: The poem is a letter, written from inside the institution where the speaker is confined. I agree with Kuklay (208-09) that, here, other female characters are implied and in the background. The "old comb" (line 2), Kuklay points out, could only have broken in a tussle among the girls.

Line 4 "Iron Ball": a special moniker for an underworld character, but there is more to it than that. No more than the [billiard] balls of line 8 have anything to do with those in "A Little Night Music," does this "Iron Ball" resemble in any way the one in 2.5 of "Van Gogh." There is, however, "Game," with its billiard balls simultaneously rolling and at a standstill. Miss I. B., a human, "rolls" (line 19). See also *Convv.* 240; and Kuklay 271 (note on "Fragment from the Golden Age").

Lines 8-9, image of two balls gently colliding, motion not continuing: this could not be billiard balls (as in "A Little Night Music"), or at most they would be metaphysical ones. The physics of billiard balls is peculiar; observation teaches us that the continuation of motion is very much the point. When one ball in motion hits another at standstill head-on, the momentum is transferred; the moving ball stops, while the standing ball starts in rolling. Thanks are due to Mark Wiedenbeck, of Altadena, California.

Lines 16-17: do these lines carry a suggestion of Raskolnikov's "perfect crime"? Is I. B. a criminal in Raskolnikov's sense? She certainly seems to know too much. Cf. JP's poem "Egy titok margójára" ("On the Margin of a Secret") (*CP* 95), lines 1-3: "Cover up well what you committed, / and after it live freely, just like / a successful assassin."

"Sketch" (143-44; 201)
A: *Kortárs* 19, no. 1 (January 1975): 84.
Comment: Kuklay 212-18; also entire section titled "Intézeti lányok" ("Girls at an Institution") (206-21).

For earlier images of the young boy, see "KZ Oratorio," "Self-Portrait from 1944," and "Auschwitz."

Lines 3-5: Kuklay (213) discourses on Hungarian *szeretet* (love in the sense of fondness, between, e.g., parents and children) versus *szerelem* (passionate love, sexual desire), a distinction English lacks. How a five-year-old would know of this important difference is a good question inside the poem. The biographical element may be another matter; JP, who grew up under the peculiar circumstances narrated in Tüskés, was no ordinary five-year-old. And that stands, even if his early relations with girls (extraordinary fondness) did not mature into successful married love (see only the note on "Love's Desert").

Line 13 "Micsicsák": possibly a made-up name for the actual girl inmate who wore said prison garment when young JP visited her at Rákospalota.

Line 14: the image is autobiographical. See the photo of five-year-old JP in Tüskés 33.

JÁNOS PILINSZKY: BIBLIOGRAPHY

There is as yet no published bibliography of János Pilinszky in any language. The listing below reflects holdings of libraries in Hungary and in the United States. A number of the entries are annotated, and abbreviations are given for sources frequently cited. Sources not actually consulted but rather cited from listings either published or unpublished are indicated by *.

1. Primary Sources

*Pilinszky, János, *Trapéz és korlát: Versek* (Trapeze and Parallel Bars: Poems). Budapest: Ezüstkor (Silver Age [monograph series]), 1946.

*——, *Aranymadár: Mesék*. Márkus Anna rajzaival (Golden Bird: Fairy Tales. With drawings by Anna Márkus). Budapest: Magvető, 1957.

*——, *Harmadnapon: Versek* (On the Third Day: Poems). Budapest: Szépirodalmi, 1959.

——, *Rekviem* (Requiem). Budapest: Magvető, 1964.
Contains: *Halak a hálóban* (Fish in a Net [Poems]): 5-37;
Rekviem (Requiem [film script]): 39-104;
Sötét mennyország: KZ-oratórium (Dark Heaven: KZ Oratorio): 105-18.
The poems, twenty-one works from "Fish in a Net" through "Metropolitan Icons," include all of the Holocaust poetry of the first three books.

——, *Nagyvárosi ikonok: Összegyűjtött versek 1940-1970* (Metropolitan Icons: Collected Poems, 1940-1970). Budapest: Szépirodalmi, 1970, ²1971.

——, *Szálkák* (Splinters). Budapest: Szépirodalmi, 1972.

——, *Végkifejlet: Versek és színművek* (Dénouement: Poems and Plays). Budapest: Szépirodalmi, 1974.
The four short plays (51-119) are: *Gyerekek és katonák* (Children and Soldiers); *Síremlék* (Grave Monument); *"Urbi et orbi" — A testi szenvedésről* ("Urbi et orbi": On Physical Suffering); and *Élőképek* (Tableaux Vivants).

——, *A nap születése*. Bálint Endre rajzaival (Birth of the Sun. With drawings by Endre Bálint). Budapest: Móra, 1974, ²1985.

*——, and Erzsébet Schaár, *Tér és kapcsolat* (Space and Connection [Poems and reproductions of sculpture]). Budapest: Magvető, 1975.

——, *Kráter: Összegyűjtött és új versek* (Crater: Collected and New Poems). Budapest: Szépirodalmi, 1976, ²1981.

—— *Válogatott művei* (Selected Works of János Pilinszky). 30 év (30 Years) series. Budapest: Magvető, Szépirodalmi, 1978.

——, *Szög és olaj: Próza* (Nail and Oil: Prose). Edited by István Jelenits. Budapest: Vigilia, 1982. (*Nail & Oil*)

——, *Beszélgetések Pilinszky Jánossal* (Conversations with János Pilinszky). Edited by Endre Török. Budapest: Magvető, 1983. (*Convv.*)

——, "Pilinszky János hagyatékából" ("From the Literary Estate of János Pilinszky") [introduced by István Jelenits], *Új Írás* (New Writing) 23, no. 12 (December 1983): 82-91.
With a photograph of the poet.

——, *A mélypont ünnepélye: Próza* (Celebration of Nadir: Prose). Edited by István Jelenits. 2 vols. Budapest: Szépirodalmi, 1984. (*Nadir*)

—— *Összegyűjtött versei* (Collected Poems of János Pilinszky). Edited by István Jelenits. Budapest: Szépirodalmi, 1987. (*CP*)
The source for the poems included and translated in this selection.

*—— *Kalandozás a tükörben: Mese* (Adventures in the Mirror: Fairy Tale). Illustrated by Katalin Irsa. Budapest: Móra, 1988.

2. *Selected Secondary Sources*

[Béládi, Miklós, et al.,] "Irodalom a gyorsuló időben: Pilinszky János költészete" ("Literature in Accelerating Time: The Poetry of J. P."), *Jelenkor* (Present Age) 24, no. 5 (May 1981): 457-68.
Panel discussion among five participants: Miklós Béládi, György Bodnár, Dezső Keresztury, Balázs Lengyel, Miklós Szabolcsi, first broadcast over Budapest Radio.

Csokits, János, "János Pilinszky's 'Desert of Love': A Note," in: Daniel Weissbort (ed.), *Translating Poetry: The Double Labyrinth* (Iowa City, IA: U of Iowa P, 1989) 9-15.

—, *Pilinszky Nyugaton: A költő 32 levelével* (P. Out West: With 32 Letters by the Poet). Budapest: Századvég Kiadó ("Fin de siècle" Publishers), 1992.

Czigány, Lóránt, "Pilinszky Nyugaton: Kiegészítések Csokits János könyvéhez" ("P. Out West: Complementary Additions to the Book by J. Cs."), *Kortárs* (Contemporary) 37, no. 7 (July 1993): 1-24.

Diószegi, András, "Pilinszky János: Szálkák" ([review of] "J. P., *Splinters*"), *Kortárs* 17, no. 10 (October 1973): 1675-79.

Domonkos, Ágnes and András Valaczka, "Pilinszky és a tárgyak" ("P. and Objects"), *Vigilia* 56, no. 7 (July 1991): 535-38.

Forgács, Rezső, "'I Want to Find My Way Home': The Last Interview with János Pilinszky," *The New Hungarian Quarterly*, no. 87 (Autumn 1982) 80-85.
    Reprinted [in Hungarian] in *Convv.* 111-22.

Fülöp, László, *Pilinszky János*. Kortársaink (Our Contemporaries) series. Budapest: Akadémiai, 1977. (Fülöp)

Gifford, Henry, "Final Realities" [review of János Pilinszky, *Selected Poems*, trans. Ted Hughes and János Csokits], *The Times Literary Supplement*, 21 January 1977 (no. 3,906) 50.

Gömöri, George, "Pilinszky, the Lonely Poet," *Hungarian Quarterly* [New York] 5, nos. 1-2 (April-June 1965): 43-47.

Görgey, Gábor, "A Pilinszky-Jambus" ("The P. Iamb"), *Jelenkor* 27, 12 (December 1984): 1137-39.

Hegyi, Béla, "Pilinszky és Rónay," in: B. H., *Kimondva is kimondatlan: Tanulmányok, kritikák* (Even Said It Is Unsaid: Essays, Reviews) (Budapest: Magvető, 1986) 62-74.

Hughes, Ted, "Postscript to János Csokits' Note," in: Daniel Weissbort (ed.), *Translating Poetry: The Double Labyrinth* (Iowa City, IA: U of Iowa P, 1989) 16-34.

Jósvai, Lidia, "Pilinszky ideje" ("P.'s Time"), *Kortárs* 37, no. 7 (July 1993): 25-31.

[Koppány, Zsolt and Zoltán Kocsis,] "'Bevallottam: a naplementét Svájcban': Koppány Zsolt beszélgetése Kocsis Zoltánnal Pilinszkyről" ("'I confessed to: sunset in Switzerland': Zs. K.'s Conversation with Z. K. about P."), *Alföld* (Lowland), 35, no. 5 (May 1984): 53-59.

Kuklay, Antal (ed.), *A kráter peremén: Gondolatok és szemelvények Pilinszky János verseihez* (On the Crater's Edge: Thoughts and Selections toward [an Understanding of] Poems by J. P.). Sárospatak: Római Katolikus Egyházi Gyűjtemény (Roman Catholic Church Collection), 1988. (Kuklay)

*Lengyel, Balázs, "A hiány költője: Pilinszky János" ("The Poet of Lack: J. P."), in: B. L., *Közelképek: Válogatott tanulmányok* (Close-Ups: Selected Essays) (Budapest: Szépirodalmi, 1979) 301-06.

Nemes Nagy, Ágnes, "János Pilinszky: A Very Different Poet (1921-1981)," *The New Hungarian Quarterly*, no. 84 (Winter 1981) 54-59. Reprinted in the 1989 edition of the Hughes-Csokits selection. See below.

——, "Versek közelről: Pilinszky János, A szerelem sivataga; Négysoros" ("Poems from Close Up: J. P., 'Love's Desert'; 'Four-Liner'"), *Jelenkor* 31, no. 12 (December 1988): 1121-25.

Németh G., Béla, "Az Apokalipszis közelében; egy ősi műfaj mai rokona: Pilinszky, Apokrif" ("Near the Apocalypse; Today's Relative of an Ancient Genre: P., 'Apocrypha'"), *Kortárs* 26, no. 9 (September 1982): 1455-65.

Pálmai, Kálmán, "A kietlenség útjain – Pilinszky Jánosról" ("On the Roads of Desolation: On J. P."), in: K. P., "Magyar líra 1970-ben" ("Hungarian Lyric Poetry in 1970"), *Irodalomtörténet* (Literary History) 53 (n.s., 3), no. 3 (1971): 560-84; 580-83.

Parker, Michael, "Hughes and the Poets of Eastern Europe," in: Keith Sagar (ed.), *The Achievement of Ted Hughes* (Athens, GA: The U of Georgia P, 1983) 37-51, and nn. (355-57).

Pomogáts, Béla, "Pilinszky János: Harbach 1944," in: B. P., *Versek közelről: Értelmezések és magyarázatok* (Poems from Close Up: Interpretations and Explications) (Budapest: Kozmosz, 1980) 141-53.

Radnóti, Sándor, "Pilinszky János lírai költészetéről" ("On J. P.'s Lyric Poetry"), in: S. R., *A szenvedő misztikus (Misztika és líra összefüggése)* (The Suffering Mystic [The Connection between Mysticism and Poetry]), Opus, Irodalomelméleti Tanulmányok (Studies in Literary Theory) series, 7 (Budapest: Akadémiai, 1981) 73-126. (S. Radnóti) Under two subheadings: "1. A szenvedő misztikus" ("The Suffering

Mystic") (73-112); "2. Formaproblémák" ("Problems of Form") (112-26).

——, "Pilinszky János meséi és drámái" (The Fairy Tales and Dramas of J.P."), *Kortárs* 18, no. 7 (July 1974): 1157-64.

Rónay, György, *Napló* (Diaries), ed. János Reisinger, 2 vols., *Rónay György Művei* (The Works of Gy. R.). Budapest: Magvető, 1989 (Rónay, *Diaries*)

The *Diaries* cover the years 1945-1952 (vol. 1) and 1953-1975 (vol. 2). With a number of entries touching on Rónay's association with Pilinszky.

——, [review of *On the Third Day*], in: Gy. R., *Olvasás közben* (While Reading) (Budapest: Magvető, 1971) 325-34.

Sanders, Ivan, "The Holocaust in Contemporary Hungarian Literature," chapter 14 in: Randolph L. Braham and Bela Vago (eds.), *The Holocaust in Hungary Forty Years Later*, East European Monographs, 190 (New York: Distributed by Columbia UP, 1985) 191-202.

Briefly discusses Miklós Radnóti and János Pilinszky as Hungary's two outstanding Holocaust poets (193-96).

[Szilágyi, János,] "János Pilinszky—A Tormented Mystic Poet: A Radio Conversation with János Pilinszky," *The New Hungarian Quarterly*, no. 77 (Spring 1980) 114-19.

Reprinted, in slightly expanded form, in *Convv.* 162-78.

Tamás, Attila, "Pilinszky János Négysoros című verséről ("On J. P.'s Poem 'Four-Liner'"), in: A. T., *Irodalom és emberi teljesség: Tanulmányok* (Literature and Human Wholeness: Essays) (Budapest: Szépirodalmi, 1973) 109-16.

Tandori, Dezső, "Egy-egy vers 'ma': Pilinszky János, Senkiföldjén" ("A Poem Here or There 'Today': J. P., 'In No Man's Land'"), *Kortárs* 24, no. 4 (April 1980): 637-40.

——, "A költői eszköztár módosulásai Pilinszky János költészetében" ("Modifications of the Store of Poetic Means in J. P.'s Poetry"), *Irodalomtörténet* 65 (n.s., 15), no. 2 (1983): 356-72. (Tandori, 1983)

——, "'A puszta súly a kuhülő kupacban': Pilinszky Jánosról" ("'Naked Weight in the Cooling Mound': On J. P."), *Kortárs* 25, no. 11 (November 1981): 1813-15.

Tüskés, Tibor, *Pilinszky János alkotásai és vallomásai tükrében* (J. P. in the

Mirror of His Creations and Confessions). Arcok és Vallomások (Faces and Confessions) series. Budapest: Szépirodalmi, 1986. (Tüskés) The only biography of János Pilinszky to date.

Vas, István, "Jó szél, magasság, mélyvíz: Déry Tibor, Pilinszky János, Parancs János" ("Good Wind, Heights, Deep Water: T. D., J. P., J. P."), in: I. V., *Az ismeretlen isten: Tanulmányok 1934-1973* (The Unknown God: Essays 1934-1973) (Budapest: Szépirodalmi, 1974) 910-21. Omnibus review. On *Metropolitan Icons*, 915-18.

Wirth, Imre, "Celan és Pilinszky" ("C. and P."), *Vigilia* 56, no. 7 (July 1991): 529-34.

3. *János Pilinszky's Work in English*

Pilinszky, János, *Selected Poems*. Translated by Ted Hughes and János Csokits. With an Introduction by Ted Hughes. Manchester: Carcanet New Press, 1976.

Published during Pilinszky's lifetime, prior to the appearance of *Crater*. Published also by Persea Books, New York. A new edition appeared in 1989 (see below).

——, *Crater: Poems 1974-5*. Translated by Peter Jay. London: Anvil Press Poetry, in association with Rex Collings, 1978.

With reproductions of sculpture by Erzsébet Schaár on the front cover, and a photograph of Pilinszky.

——, *The Desert of Love: Selected Poems*. Translated by János Csokits and Ted Hughes, introduced by Ted Hughes, with a memoir by Ágnes Nemes Nagy. [Revised and enlarged edition.] London: Anvil Press Poetry, 1989.

——, *66 Poems / Pilinszky János, 66 vers*. Translated by István Tótfalusi. n.p. [Budapest:] Maecenas Könyvkiadó, 1991.

——, *Wüstenei der Liebe / The Desert of Love*. [Poems in English and in German translation.] Translated by Hans-Henning Paetzke, Eva Czjzek, János Csokits, Ted Hughes, et al. Ho Libri series. Budapest: Kossuth, 1992.

—, *Conversations with Sheryl Sutton: The Novel of a Dialogue.* Translated by Peter Jay and Éva Major. Manchester: Carcanet; Budapest: Corvina, 1992.

4. *Reference Works Cited*

Columbia Dictionary of Modern European Literature. Edited by Jean-Albert Bede and William B. Edgerton. 2nd ed. rev. and enl. New York: Columbia UP, 1980. (*CDMEL*)

Der Insel-Verlag: Eine Bibliographie 1899-1969. Compiled and edited by Heinz Sarkowski. Frankfurt am Main: Insel, 1970. (Sarkowski)

Kortárs Magyar Írók Kislexikona, 1959-1988 (Shorter Dictionary of Contemporary Hungarian Writers, 1959-1988). Edited by István Fazakas. Budapest: Magvető, 1989. (*KMÍK*)

Magyar Életrajzi Lexikon (Hungarian Biographical Dictionary). Edited by Ágnes Kenyeres. 3 vols. Budapest: Akadémiai, [4]1967, [2]1981, 1981. (*MÉL*)

ABOUT THE TRANSLATOR

Emery George was born in Budapest in 1933, and came to the United States in 1946. At the University of Michigan, in Ann Arbor, where he is professor emeritus of German, he has taught courses in Hungarian poetry and poetics; he has also lectured at numerous institutions of higher learning, including Boston, Brown, Columbia, Indiana, and Yale Universities. Mr. George's many translations from contemporary Hungarian literature include a translated edition of the complete poetry of Miklós Radnóti, poems by numerous other Hungarian poets (including Lajos Kassák, Gyula Illyés, István Vas, and Sándor Weöres), and István Eörsi's *His Master's Voice*, a two-act play based on the life and work of Georg Lukács. They have appeared in such periodicals as *Chicago Review, The Kenyon Review, The Literary Review, Partisan Review*; the yearbook *Cross Currents*; and the anthologies *Against Forgetting, Anthology of Magazine Verse, New Directions in Prose and Poetry*, and *Voices within the Ark*. Mr. George's other work includes seven collections of his own poetry; the most recent of these, *Blackbird: A Book of Poems on the World and Work of Franz Kafka*, is also available from the Edwin Mellen Press.

STUDIES IN SLAVIC LANGUAGE AND LITERATURE